DIRECTORS
THE ALL-TIME GREATS

Steven Spielberg directs **Indiana Jones and The Temple of Doom** *(1984).*

DIRECTORS
THE ALL-TIME GREATS

NEIL SINYARD

COLUMBUS BOOKS
LONDON

Contents

This book was devised and produced by
Multimedia Publications (UK) Ltd

Editor: Richard Rosenfeld
Assistant editors: Graham Fuller,
                 Sydney Francis
 Production: Arnon Orbach
Design: Michael Hodson Designs
Picture Research: Veneta Bullen

Copyright © Multimedia Publications (UK)
Ltd 1985

Sinyard, Neil
Directors: The All Time Greats
1. Moving pictures producers and directors
i Title
791.43'0233'0922 PN1998.A2
ISBN No. 0 86287 259 6

First published in the United States of
America 1985 by Gallery Books, an imprint
of W. H. Smith Publishers Inc.,
112 Madison Avenue, New York, NY 10016

First published in the United Kingdom 1985
by Columbus Books, Devonshire House,
29 Elmsfield Road, Bromley, Kent BR1 1LT
ISBN 0 86287 259 6

Typeset by Letterspace and Elements
Origination by The Clifton Studio Ltd, London
Printed in Italy by Sagdos

This page: *David Lean (fourth from right) on location for* **A Passage to India** *(1984).*

Endpapers: *Stanley Kubrick (in front of ladder) shoots* **Spartacus** *(1960).*

Page 1: *Erich von Stroheim directs* **Greed** *(1923).*

1 The Pioneers

This book outlines the careers of some of the greatest film-makers in screen history. The survey covers four particular categories of director: those pioneers who established their reputations during the silent period, up to about 1929; the Hollywood stylists and storytellers who flourished within the studio system between 1930 and 1960; the artists who may be said to have made an important contribution to the acceptance of film as an art form; and modern film-makers whose reputations have been made in the period after 1960.

The divisions are not meant to be mutually exclusive. Nearly all the silent film-makers did significant work in the sound era. A number of Hollywood film-makers can certainly be regarded as artists on a par with their European counterparts, though, as the introductions to the chapters will indicate, it is a different kind of artistry and has found a different kind of recognition. Because this selection cannot hope to be comprehensive, my choice has been guided by a sense of film history, which necessitates certain inclusions, and by personal taste.

A job of work?

Without following a strict formula in describing the directors' careers, I have tried to give a sense of their development, the things that particularly characterize their films in terms of theme and style, and an indication of their recognition by their peers and by the public. I have summarized what have been generally considered to be their strengths and weaknesses, though I have not hesitated to attempt a different approach to their work if aspects of their careers seem to me to have been understated or misunderstood. In describing their work in this way, I have

Left: *Fritz Lang at work, lining up a shot. Lang worked with equal distinction in both the silent and sound era of the cinema, in Germany and in Hollywood.*

tried to imply something of the personality behind the films. Some directors would play down the relevance of this and say that, to them, directing a film is simply a job of work and has nothing to do with their personal beliefs. But behind my career descriptions of each of them is the suggestion that, as the distinguished director Rouben Mamoulian put it, "The films of a great director are always autobiographical..."

Right: *Man of destiny. Albert Dieudonné appears in the title role of Abel Gance's technically ambitious epic of the silent era,* **Napoléon** *(1926).*

Above: *King Vidor (right of camera) prepares an elaborate shot for the Coney Island sequence in* **The Crowd** *(1929), in which the camera will slide down in front of the actors.*

Right: *A striking composition from* **Greed**, *Erich von Stroheim's mutilated but still masterly adaptation of Frank Norris' novel "McTeague".*

Playing at God

Most of the great directors have very different conceptions of their roles. Producer-director Stanley Kramer once divided directors into two types: those who think they are God; and those who *know* they are God. But there are at least 57 other varieties.

Some directors see their role as that of a team-member; others as the captain of a team; still others as the *owner* of a team. According to circumstance or personality, or both, a director's role can veer between autocrat or democrat, composer or conductor, front-line general or assembly-line employee, creative artist or deferential interpreter. In the final analysis (i.e. at the premiere), he can be hero or fall-guy.

The silent dawn

In the cinema's age of innocence, as the film historian Kevin Brownlow said, all the film director needed to be able to do was shout. He could treat material as if it were on a stage and simply arrange entrances and exits for the actors, while the camera recorded this process from beginning to end. In these early days, the director was not really a specialist. Apart from the acting, he did more or less everything himself and was the equivalent of a modern studio. He did not need education, only youth, enthusiasm and a basic visual sense. At around this time, directors like Charles Chaplin and D.W. Griffith did not work from scripts, but carried the whole film in their head – which, given the length and complexity of a work like Griffith's *Intolerance* (1916), was quite a feat.

The period between about 1914 and 1924 was perhaps the greatest era of freedom for the film director, though few exploited this fully. It was a time before the cinema had become completely industrialized, so the director was comparatively free from having to satisfy the rival claims of box-office, stars, censorship, producers and studio. A turning point was reached with the profligacy of Erich von Stroheim on *Greed* (1925) and the cutting of the film by MGM, after which the freedom of the director was either curtailed or more closely watched. Yet some still found a way to express their personal vision with the minimum of interference.

Reality and dream

As the language of the cinema became more sophisticated, it became clear that, for most directors, it offered the choice of two possibilities: between the camera's ability to photograph real life; or, conversely, its ability to transcend reality and create a world of its own. For a director like Robert Flaherty, the cinema offered a technical opportunity for capturing on film a reality or lifestyle about which we may otherwise have been ignorant. His film about Eskimo life, *Nanook of the North* (1922), represents the birth of the documentary before the word itself had been coined. Along with Stroheim's *Greed*, King Vidor's war drama *The Big Parade* (1925) and his contemporary tragedy about a typical urban man, *The Crowd* (1928), *Nanook* brought an intense realism to the screen, holding up a mirror to nature so that audiences could see a heightened reflection of their own lives.

On the other hand, F.W. Murnau's horror classic *Nosferatu, the Vampyre* (1923) and Abel Gance's historical epic *Napoleon* (1926) were works of pure imagination and fantasy, exploiting the cinema's capacity for dazzling visual effects. In Cecil B. DeMille's biblical dramas, *The Ten Commandments* (1923) and *The King of Kings* (1927), cinema became an extraordinarily successful combination of sermon and spectacle, disdained by the intelligentsia but adored by the public.

The early giants

Film as magic carpet, or film as window on the world: to some extent, the choice between these two extremes has remained the same throughout the cinema's history. What was different for the pioneers was the newness of the medium; the possibility for experimentation and innovation; and the near certainty of a mass audience for their efforts. The great silent directors explored the expressive potential of their medium and simultaneously created a permanent memorial of their art and philosophy. In Griffith, one senses the cinema's capacity for inspiring universal brotherhood. In Chaplin, one feels its ability to reveal the pathos of poverty and the resilience of the human spirit. Sergei M. Eisenstein discovers the cinema's potential for political polemic, while Fritz Lang develops its language to display the terrors of a technological society. Buster Keaton simply raises film slapstick to the level of choreographic art. Through giants like these, the history of the cinema got off to a flying start.

Charles Chaplin (1889-1977)

Charlie Chaplin was the cinema's first Everyman. Deriving from Chaplin's own impoverished childhood in Victorian England, the figure of the Tramp represents one of society's victims – but one who never refuses to submit to his fate, which is the reason that audiences found him moving as well as funny. As a director, Chaplin was unoriginal, but his overall contribution to the cinema's mythology and conscience is so great as to be incalculable.

He had a simple rule for direction: long-shot for comedy, close-up for sentiment. The long-shot provided the detachment necessary for humor. In a routine like the nonsense song in *Modern Times* (1936), it allowed space for Chaplin to exhibit his balletic grace as a performer. The camera moved in when a crucial emotional point was being made, like the final close-up of *City Lights* (1931) when Charlie reveals his identity to the blind girl whose sight has been restored and, amazed, she recognizes her benefactor as a tramp.

Chaplin's reputation was made during the silent era through such marvellous sequences as the meal of boots and laces in *The Gold Rush* (1925), which shows the Tramp's ability to create something sustaining out of something appalling through sheer will of imagination. The Tramp's eloquent silent mime was gradually to fade out of Chaplin's repertoire as he adjusted to the coming of sound, the turning-point being the overt verbal denunciation of Fascism that so stunningly concludes *The Great Dictator* (1940).

Above: *A production still from Chaplin's last picture,*
The Countess from Hong Kong (1966), in which Sophia Loren
(right) co-starred with Marlon Brando.

Center: *Chaplin appears as Adenoid Hynkel, dictator of Tomania,*
in The Great Dictator (1940), a black comedy satire that bravely
attacked Hitler and the Nazi menace.

Far left: *Charles Chaplin gets ready to shoot a scene from one of*
his classic silent comedies, The Gold Rush (1925).

In fact, the social protest that under-
lay Chaplin's creation of the Tramp was
to become more controversial in later
films. In *Modern Times*, theft by the
poor is seen as a justifiable answer to
starvation in Depression America. In
the extraordinary *Monsieur Verdoux*
(1947) – outspoken, uncomfortable, but
an unqualified masterpiece – Chaplin's
Bluebeard murderer sees his crimes
as paltry and even morally defensible
in comparison with the brutality of big
business, the pomposity of power politics, the insanity of world war.

Rags-to-riches story

There was always a strong element of
autobiography in Chaplin's work. The
progress from rags to riches in *The Gold
Rush*, yet the reassurance that he can
still be loved for himself, stems from
his own personal experience. So, too,
does the nostalgic evocation of music
hall and London in 1914 in *Limelight*
(1952) and the sour re-creation of
McCarthyist America in *A King in New
York* (1957), which chillingly recalls
Chaplin's exile from America for his
socialist beliefs.

The seemingly unending struggles
between wealth and poverty, love and
sacrifice, rebellion and servility, always animated Chaplin's films. The
Tramp's clinging to his ragged trousers
was really a mime in miniature of the
individual's instinctive hold on his
own dignity, and was just one example
of the way Chaplin, with a gesture,
could turn tears of laughter to those of
poignant recognition. His performing
gifts alone would establish him as one
of the comic geniuses of modern times,
but the social range and rage of that
comedy put him in a class by himself.

Sergei M. Eisenstein (1898-1948)

Above: *Sergei Eisenstein (seated) directs Nikolai Cherkasov in the title role of* **Ivan the Terrible** *(1944-46). Eisenstein's regular cinematographer, Eduard Tisse, is behind the camera.*

Sergei M. Eisenstein was always grateful to the Russian Revolution. It gave him the freedom to decide what to do with his life and made an artist out of him. It also gave him the subject for his early, epoch-making films. What is remarkable about these works is not the message but the method. Film-makers who might reject Eisenstein's ideas were nevertheless overwhelmed by his technique.

Eisenstein's method was basically an exercise in shock tactics. He used the camera not as the eyes of an objective witness but as a fist with which to strike an audience out of complacency. His editing is not simply the means by which he tells a story on film: it overlays the plot with a clearly defined political attitude. For example, he not only shows strikers being massacred in *Strike* (1925): he cross-cuts the sequence with shots of animals being slaughtered in an abattoir to heighten the horror and make an audience share his outrage at political butchery.

The most awesome example of Eisenstein's technique in action is the Odessa Steps sequence from *Battleship Potemkin* (1925), in which a troop of Cossack soldiers open fire on innocent civilians. The scene is a mosaic of confusion and chaos, created through a calculated alternation of light and dark, upward and downward movement, individual anguish and mass panic. In sharing the innocent people's feelings of horror and helplessness, an audience becomes caught up in the struggle of the mass against the tyranny of their rulers, and their prolonged scream of pain and anger against brutal oppression. That moment makes revolutionaries of us all. It should be said that, for all his intellectual theorizing, Eisenstein was one of the cinema's most adroit directors of spectacle. The storming of the Winter Palace in *October/Ten Days That Shook the World* (1928) is another comparably stirring sequence, and a visual masterpiece.

12

Eisenstein's exile

Eisenstein's great creative period was the twenties, when the aftermath of the Revolution had stimulated excitement and experimentation in all varieties of Soviet art. Unfortunately for Eisenstein, the following decade was full of frustration, with an abortive period in Hollywood and a number of unfulfilled projects in his own country. He returned to international eminence with *Alexander Nevsky* (1938) and the two-part *Ivan the Terrible* (1944-6), historical films on a grand scale, with majestic set-pieces (like the battle on the ice in *Alexander Nevsky*) and scores by Prokofiev that set new standards in film music.

It is difficult to separate the aesthete from the propagandist in Eisenstein, but there is no doubt about his stature and significance. "Of all the arts," said Lenin, "for us the cinema is the most important." In Soviet Russia its most important voice was Eisenstein. In finding filmic forms to express collectivism and brotherhood, he gave substance to a national ideology.

Above: *An anguished mother carries her murdered child in a dramatic detail from Eisenstein's most famous set-piece, the Odessa Steps massacre in* **Battleship Potemkin** *(1925).*

Left: *A still from Eisenstein's last film,* **Ivan the Terrible**. *The second part was sharply criticized by the Soviet authorities and not released until 1958.*

Left: *The father of the modern cinema, D. W. Griffith, directs a scene from **The Struggle** (1931), his final film.*

Above: *A shot from Griffith's massive re-creation of ancient Babylon, whose destruction is one of the four stories of his epic, **Intolerance** (1916).*

D. W. Griffith (1875 - 1948)

"Remember David Wark Griffith," said Alfred Hitchcock, when Griffith died in 1948. "Every time you go to the cinema you enjoy, in some indirect but plainly traceable form, the fruits of his labors." After an unsuccessful early career as a dramatist, poet and actor, Griffith had joined the Biograph Company, become a film director and made about 150 films in five years before his extravagance and Biograph's restrictions forced a parting of the ways in 1913. Within two years, Griffith was to make perhaps the most celebrated of all silent films, *The Birth of a Nation* (1915).

"History written in lightning" was President Woodrow Wilson's description of this massive saga of the American Civil War and its aftermath. It was the *Gone With the Wind* of its day, with staggering photography by Griffith's regular cameraman Billy Bitzer and superb battle scenes. But its ambiguous portrayal of the Ku Klux Klan provoked controversy and attempted suppression that shocked Griffith. Partially to vindicate himself against the accusations of bigotry, he embarked on an even larger project, *Intolerance* (1916), a three-hour epic that intertwined four stories illus-

trating various forms of intolerance through the ages. It was not as successful as *The Birth of a Nation* with public or critics, though most film historians regard it as a finer work and directors like Sergei M. Eisenstein and Vsevolod Pudovkin were enormously influenced by its techniques.

Apart from *Broken Blossoms* (1919) and *Way Down East* (1920), Griffith's later films are comparatively undistinguished, and his career ended in a prolonged, drink-sodden decline. His films have been attacked as old-fashioned Victorian melodrama, too much preoccupied with damsels (mainly Lillian Gish) in distress: there is more modernity and movement, say his critics, in the speed and panache of the Keystone Kops.

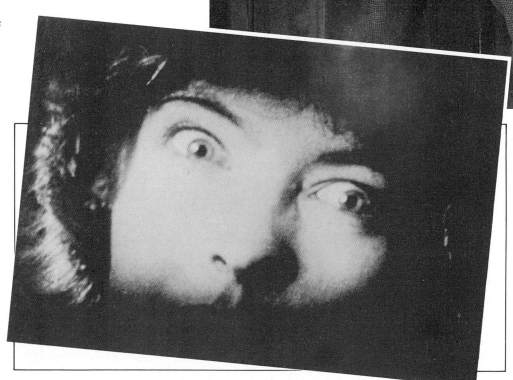

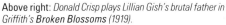

Above right: *Donald Crisp plays Lillian Gish's brutal father in Griffith's* Broken Blossoms *(1919).*

Below right: *An example of Griffith's dramatic use of close-up, as Lillian Gish is cornered in* Broken Blossoms.

Cinema's first stylist

For many, however, Griffith is the inventor of the language of the cinema. The use of such devices as close-up, deep-focus, split-screen, dissolves, which are part of the natural vocabulary of modern cinema, were all taken to daring extremes by Griffith. He popularized feature-length narrative; alerted audiences to the potential of film for political propaganda; stunned fellow film-makers with the revelation of the creative possibilities of montage, and encouraged a new subtlety and realism in screen performance. Above all, he was the first figure in film history to give this new mass medium intellectual respectability. *The Birth of a Nation* is seen by some as the birth of the cinema. It is not: it is the birth of an art form.

Buster Keaton (1895 - 1966)

Buster Keaton died just after the critical revaluation of his work had begun but too early to know how comprehensive this reassessment would be. He is now regarded as the finest of the silent comedians, and *The General* (1926) as the finest of all silent comedies (indeed the best film ever made about the American Civil War). As early as 1927, in a review of Keaton's *College*, the great European director Luis Buñuel was extolling the virtues of Keaton's crisp, matter-of-fact style over the more ponderous Germanic manner favored at the time, but it took 40 years for the critical establishment to rally in support of such praise.

Unlike Chaplin, Keaton is never interested in the whys and whats of a situation: he is mostly interested in how. The emphasis is on motion more than emotion. The great joy of the films is in the natural nonchalance that Keaton brings to the most hair-raising piece of comedy, like his staggering jump across the waterfall to rescue his girl in *Our Hospitality* (1923), or the serene stillness with which he experi-ences the collapse of his home around his ears during a hurricane in *Steamboat Bill, Jr* (1928).

Mechanical Marvel

He has been called the master of the deadpan, but his body was a mechanical marvel, and his face was as expressive as any of the great screen actors ("When he moved his eyes," said the critic James Agee, "it was like seeing them move in a statue.") He never mugged at the camera to gain audience sympathy and his modest manhood vindicated itself through logic and resourcefulness rather than sentiment and strength.

Perhaps this very modestly explains the underestimation of Keaton for so long. As a director and actor, he paid the penalty for making it all look so real, so natural. But his films contain astonishing things. There is, for example, the sequence in *Sherlock, Jr* (1924) where, as a cinema projectionist, he dreams himself into the film he is showing and is threatened by rapid montage and changes of scene; or the shot in *The General*, where, without fakery, we see a train falling through a bridge (allegedly the most expensive single take in the silent cinema); or the vision of social chaos in *Cops* (1922), where the innocent Keaton is progressively chased by the entire city police force. Keaton's comedy owed little to music hall and everything to a quintessentially cinematic skill in using every inch of the film frame for full effect. To this day, fellow directors like Richard Lester freely marvel at and learn from Keaton's supreme visual economy.

Above: Setting up a mechanical gag, one of Keaton's specialities.

Left: Buster Keaton, in a thoughtful mood, during a break between takes.

Below: Keaton takes the helm in **The Navigator** (1924), one of the greatest of his feature-length comedies.

Above: At the swimming baths, Buster fails to impress his girl with his sporting prowess in **The Cameraman** (1928).

Right: Keaton relaxes behind the camera prior to excelling in front of it.

Fritz Lang
(1890 - 1976)

Born in Vienna, Fritz Lang made some of the greatest German silent films, most famously *Metropolis* (1926). Propaganda minister Joseph Goebbels was so impressed that he suggested Lang should take charge of the Third Reich's film industry. But Lang left Germany at Hitler's accession to power, having just completed an extraordinary film about a hunt for a child murderer, *M* (1931). Its portrait of pre-war Germany – the beggars, the identity cards, the incipient hysteria – offers a frightening premonition of the atmosphere developing in that country.

Although Lang subsequently settled in America and began a new career, this Germanic sense of anxiety and doom never left his work. His first American film, *Fury* (1936), contains the seeds of everything to follow: an indictment of mob rule, which almost leads to the lynching of an innocent man; a hero set on vengeance who becomes corrupted and perverted in the pursuit of his vendetta; an overall atmosphere of paranoia and overwhelming fate. A baroque western like *Rancho Notorious* (1952) and a violent gangster film like *The Big Heat* (1953) – famous for the moment when the gangster's moll has scalding coffee thrown in her face – are continuations of the familiar pattern of hate, murder and revenge in Lang.

Torment and guilt

In Lang's films, characters are always on trial and the courtroom becomes a torture chamber of guilt in which the accused sees himself as prosecutor and judge. "I am always forced to move along streets and someone is always behind me," says Peter Lorre's wretched child-murderer in *M*. "It is I, I am myself behind me – and yet I cannot escape." Two Edward G. Robinson performances – as a Professor implicated in murder in *The Woman in the Window* (1944), and as an undervalued artist who becomes infatuated with a prostitute in *Scarlet Street* (1945) – embody to perfection the tormented

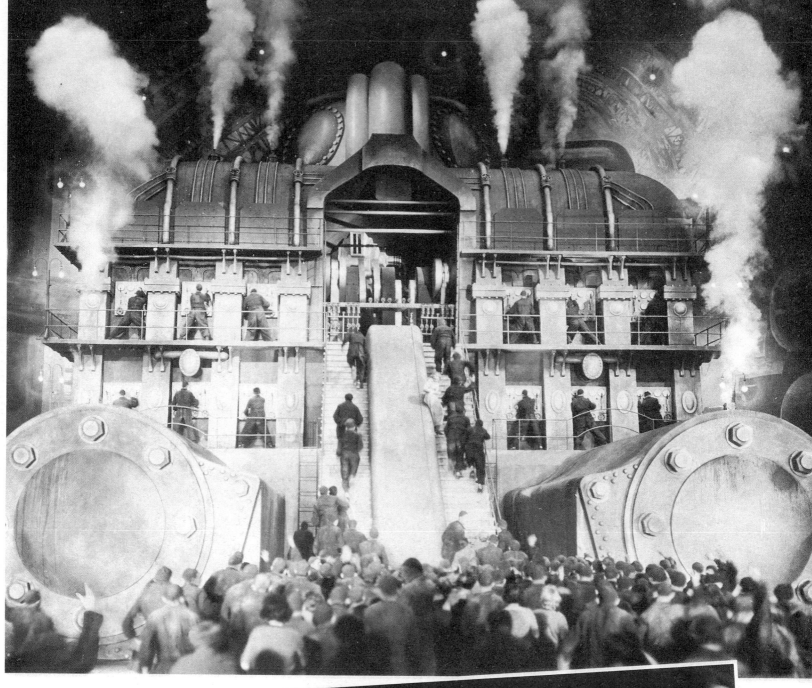

Right: *A dramatic detail from Lang's first American film,* Fury *(1936) – a member of the lynch mob prepares to go into action.*

Lang hero, trapped by personality, circumstance and environment.

Lang's vision is a forbidding one, but it has a particular resonance for anyone who feels, like him, the tragic insignificance of today's individual in the face of global, social and psychological forces over which he has no control. Lang's presentation of fear and alienation in the modern city influenced film-makers like Alfred Hitchcock, Stanley Kubrick and Jean-Luc Godard. *Metropolis* is the father of countless science-fiction extravaganzas, and Lang's forties thrillers chillingly instil European nightmare into Hollywood optimism. Lang was truly an apocalyptic child of the twentieth century, wondering if we would ever make it to the twenty-first.

The situation of the director during the heyday of Hollywood has often been seen in terms of the struggle of the individual against the system. It was never really like that. For one thing, many Hollywood directors were quite happy working as a hired hand, of roughly equal status to the writer and lower than that of producer or star. For another, the studio system had its strengths as well as its weaknesses. Freedom from studio interference did not necessarily guarantee a great film. Conversely, films that were clearly cooperative studio enterprises – such as *Casablanca* (1943) and *Singin' in the Rain* (1952) – endure as classic movies.

Above: *Perched on a ladder, Vincente Minnelli checks a set-up for the MGM musical,* **Brigadoon** *(1953), with two cameras ready to cover the scene. Joseph Ruttenberg is the cameraman.*

Above right: *Lana Turner (seated, center) is surrounded by gentlemen admirers in a scene from Minnelli's film about Hollywood,* **The Bad and the Beautiful** *(1952). Walter Pidgeon prepares to pour the champagne.*

Right: *James Dean (center) embraces his two teenage friends, Sal Mineo (left) and Natalie Wood (right), in a moment from Nicholas Ray's* **Rebel Without a Cause** *(1955).*

The stamp of greatness

The great Hollywood directors were men who succeeded within the system and yet were able to put their own personal stamp on a film. In some cases, this required a certain amount of maneuver or resilience. John Ford minimized studio tampering with his films by cutting in the camera and by being so rude to any studio representative sent to chastize him that it was generally felt advisable to leave him alone. William Wyler made many memorable films for producer Samuel Goldwyn but he also had many fights with him. "I made *Wuthering Heights*," Goldwyn used to insist, "Wyler only directed it." In order to eliminate this source of harassment, Wyler finally chose to produce as well as direct his own films.

Orson Welles summed up the problem this way: "In England, a producer is a man who stages a play; on Broadway, he is the man who finances a play; in Hollywood, he is the man who interferes with a movie." This was not entirely true, since there were many creative producers in Hollywood at the time: David O. Selznick, who produced *Gone With the Wind* (1939); John Houseman, who worked with Vincente Minnelli on such films as *The Bad and the Beautiful* (1952) and *Lust for Life* (1956); and Ross Hunter, who collaborated with Douglas Sirk on a number of fine melodramas, to name but a few.

Certainly the big studio bosses, like Louis B. Mayer of MGM, Jack Warner of Warner Brothers and Harry Cohn of Columbia, had their notorious idiosyncrasies. Mayer was a conservative sentimentalist famous for his weeping displays and his use of emotional blackmail on employees. Warner was reputedly so mean that he would tour the studio late at night to ensure that all the lights in the toilets had been switched off. The foul-mouthed Harry Cohn, meanwhile, apparently not only knew nothing about art, he could not even recite the Lord's Prayer. But if the moguls were artistically ignorant, they were also sharp businessmen who loved movies and knew audiences. For all their quirks, they were respected for that. "He wasn't in the money business," said director Robert Aldrich of Harry Cohn, "he was in the movie business." Moreover, the studio system was very efficient, had superlative

Storytellers

technicians and ensured continuity of production. Directors knew who they had to deal with, and the surviving veterans now look back with nostalgia on those days. After all, it was easier talking to even Louis B. Mayer than to a conglomerate.

Going it alone

Change was inevitable, and it started after World War II. Making a bid for more creative freedom, some directors went into independent production with varying degrees of success. The changing habits of film-going audiences also inevitably necessitated a change in film production. In the golden years of the studio system, superslick Hollywood pros like Michael Curtiz, the director of *Casablanca* and many Errol Flynn action films, or Raoul Walsh, who made classic gangster movies with James Cagney and Humphrey Bogart, could each turn out four or five films a year. But today a director who averages one film a year is prolific and it has taken an established director like Fred Zinnemann 20 years to make his last five pictures.

The TV revolution

The fifties was a particularly traumatic time for the industry. Hollywood was shaken by the McCarthy witch-hunt. Some talented people were blacklisted and left for Europe, like Charles Chaplin and Joseph Losey. Others, such as Robert Rossen, recanted but never rediscovered the vigor of their early work.

Above: *Ben Gazzara (behind bars) plays a soldier on trial for his life in Otto Preminger's **Anatomy of a Murder** (1959).*

Hollywood's response to the impact of television also had its effect on directors, who were under pressure to develop those cinematic facilities that television could not at that time provide – color, wide-screen, and more controversial subject matter. Most directors hated the wide-screen, thinking its shape was only suitable for filming duck-shoots or dachshunds, and not permitting the kind of concentrated detail a director had formerly required. "You can't get a close-up of a finger-nail," commented Alfred Hitchcock disdainfully. For a director like Nicholas Ray, however, all these challenges yielded a fine film like *Rebel Without a Cause* (1955), which expressively uses color and screen width and is enduringly perceptive on the problems of youth.

A number of directors revelled in the more liberal atmosphere. Otto Preminger made one of the best ever courtroom dramas, *Anatomy of a Murder* (1959), from subject matter that a few years before would not have made the screen. When directors from television graduated to film-making, like John Frankenheimer, Sidney Lumet and Martin Ritt, they brought their television techniques with them. Television was to prove a useful training-ground for aspiring film-makers, but it continued to eat into the audience.

Unlikely authors

Perhaps most extraordinarily, some Hollywood directors suddenly found themselves thrust into artistic eminence. Critics writing for the French film magazine *Cahiers du Cinéma* and the American critic Andrew Sarris minted a novel word for those skilled directors who had created a thematically or intellectually consistent body of work – *auteur*, or "author". This variously amused, gratified and ex-

Left: *Laurence Olivier, as Heathcliff, is apprehended in the gardens of Thrushcross Grange in a scene from the Sam Goldwyn/William Wyler film of **Wuthering Heights** (1939). David Niven (center) looks on.*

asperated the Hollywood directors themselves, who felt that they were sometimes credited with insights they were completely unaware of. Nevertheless, despite their excesses, the auteurist critics did discover and celebrate major works that had hitherto been ignored or blandly accepted as routine Hollywood product. Examples include John Ford's *The Searchers* (1956) and Alfred Hitchcock's *Vertigo* (1958), both now widely held to be masterpieces.

Although it does not disqualify them from being artists, none of the directors in the following section saw themselves as such, with the possible exception of Orson Welles. All of them saw film primarily as a mass medium rather than an art form. They made films for audiences, not for themselves, and – again with the exception of Welles – they mostly subscribed to the idea of an invisible camera style that did not obstruct the story or alert an audience to a presence behind the camera. At the same time they all loved and took their craft seriously. All of these directors had a point to make but it was mostly hidden under an absorbing narrative. Nevertheless, as these career descriptions show, that point can be uncovered to enhance our enjoyment.

Above: *The camera crew for the Samuel Bronston production, Nicholas Ray's* **55 Days at Peking** *(1962), moves in for a take of the Band Concert sequence.*

Below: *Nicholas Ray prepares to direct Ava Gardner in a scene from* **55 Days at Peking**.

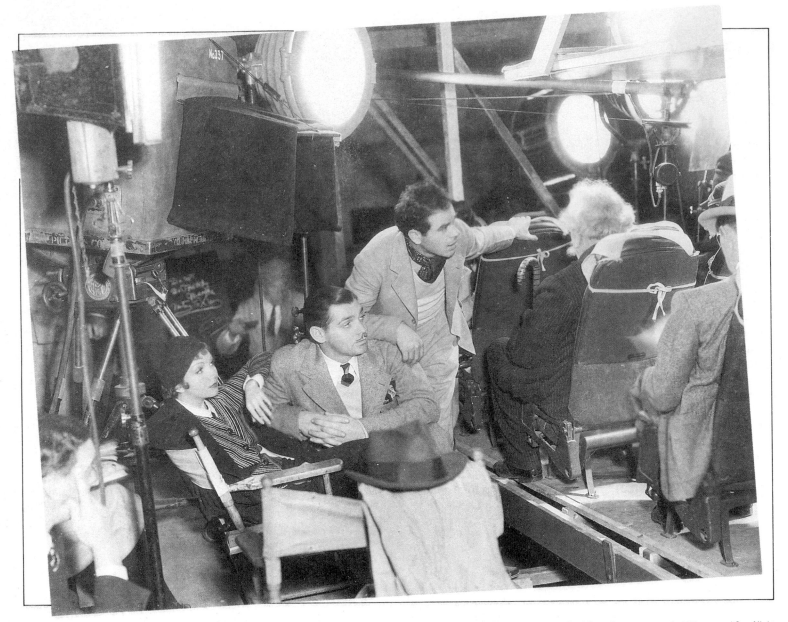

Above: *Frank Capra lines up a scene for* It Happened One Night *(1934), with Claudette Colbert (seated left) and Clark Gable (center). All three won Oscars for the film.*

Frank Capra (1897 -)

Frank Capra called his autobiography *The Name Above the Title*. It is his immodest reminder of his former eminence in Hollywood. It also proclaims his pride at his rise from poor Sicilian immigrant during his childhood to one of the great popular film-makers by the end of the thirties.

Capra won three directing Oscars in the space of five years, for *It Happened One Night* (1934), *Mr Deeds Goes to Town* (1936), and *You Can't Take It With You* (1938). During this period, he also made *Lost Horizon* (1937) and *Mr Smith Goes to Washington* (1939). These films represent the height of Capra's achievement and the synthesis of his beliefs.

David and Goliath

Capra's major films were comedies with a strong moral lesson, and their message of optimism over adversity cheered up audiences during the Depression. His films were essentially variations on David and Goliath, with the common man victorious over seemingly insurmountable odds. His main characters, like Mr Deeds (Gary Cooper) or Mr Smith (James Stewart), were innocent idealists who, by example, converted the cynics and, by strength of will, vanquished the crooks, those figures of power and wealth who put economics above humanity.

Capra never recovered his popularity after World War II, and his bitter feud with the star Glenn Ford on *Pocketful of Miracles* (1961) hastened his retirement. His testament is the aptly entitled *It's a Wonderful Life* (1946), a beautiful fantasy on the typical Capra theme that no man is born a failure, and starring James Stewart as another famous Capra hero.

Some dismiss his work as "Capracorn". Others hail his sense of comic pace and his Dickensian flair for colorful characterization. John Ford nicely described Capra as "an inspiration to those who believe in the American Dream". Ironically, the spirit of America has recently swung back Capra's way, but is there anyone of Capra's talent to exploit it?

George Cukor (1899-1983)

George Cukor's films had that indefinable touch of class. They respected and relished good dialogue. Visually, they did not show off. Dramatically, they were an actor's paradise. Greta Garbo in *Camille* (1937), Ingrid Bergman in *Gaslight* (1944) and Judy Garland in *A Star Is Born* (1954) are only some of the great performances in Cukor films.

Cukor came to Hollywood from directing on the New York stage. This theatrical background is an important clue to his work. A number of his films are adaptations of plays, and Cukor was always intrigued by theatrical people indulging a flair for the dramatic, either on stage or in a courtroom. He was a shrewd observer of the importance and attraction of role-playing in everyday life, and the alternately comic and tragic split between a person's double life in public and in private.

Gaslight and tights

Cukor's films were more about feeling than action. His one Western, *Heller in Pink Tights* (1960), was about the theater, not the West. The only war films he made were about the sex war. These were either disturbing dramas about masculine domination, like *A Woman's Face* (1941) or *Gaslight*, or sprightly Spencer Tracy – Katharine Hepburn comedies like *Adam's Rib* (1949) and *Pat and Mike* (1952), which debate feminist issues ahead of their time. No one who has seen the musical numbers of *A Star Is Born*, or the passionate response to the atmosphere of India in *Bhowani Junction* (1956), could doubt Cukor as a visual stylist, but one remembers his films mostly for the performances. Spencer Tracy never looked greater than in his films for Cukor; even the cat in *The Actress* (1953) acts superbly. Cukor's Oscar for Best Director came for his last major film, *My Fair Lady* (1964) – in honor, one feels, for his whole career.

Top right: *George Cukor (right) rehearses his actors.*

Right: *Audrey Hepburn as Eliza Doolittle in the film that won Cukor his Oscar, My Fair Lady (1964).*

John Ford (1895 - 1973)

"A poet, a comedian", was Orson Welles' description of John Ford. The comic is revealed in the raucous, rollicking horseplay of the supporting characters. The poet expresses himself through the use of the camera, the instinctive manner in which Ford can frame his characters against landscape to suggest their aspirations, potential and destiny.

John Ford won more Oscars than any other director – for *The Informer* (1935), *The Grapes of Wrath* (1940), *How Green Was My Valley* (1941), *The Quiet Man* (1952), as well as a couple for his war documentaries. Ironically, not one of those was for a Western, the genre with which Ford is most associated. In 1939 *Stagecoach* united Ford with the magnificent landscape of Monument Valley and the great screen presence of John Wayne (they had been around before, but not like this). Thereafter the combination of director, actor and setting was cemented in the cavalry trilogy, *Fort Apache* (1948), *She Wore a Yellow Ribbon* (1949), and *Rio Grande* (1950), films about comradeship, adventure, patriotism and the responsibilities of command. A different atmosphere pervades *The Searchers* (1956), a tragic story of a loner that was to become one of Ford's most discussed and influential films and that would usher in a darker tone to his subsequent work.

Hard-nosed director

Ford made a pretence of simplicity. "I'm just a hard-nosed director," he said. "I get a script – if I like it, I'll do it". But this impression of artlessness does not tally with the kind of conscious craftsmanship that produces the lyrical dance sequence of *My Darling Clementine* (1946); the poetic final shots of *The Searchers*; or even Ford's insistence that the cast of *Cheyenne Autumn* (1964) stand out in the sun until he had exactly the length of shadow he wanted.

There is much complexity and feeling behind his films. They are about community and the endurance of the common people, but they also confront prejudice, injustice, and the tragedy of destroyed families. His Westerns celebrate America's past but they also show the cost of progress and the shaky basis of some of the nation's myths. Still, as the newspaper editor says in one of Ford's masterpieces, *The Man Who Shot Liberty Valance* (1962): "This is the West, sir. When the legend becomes fact, print the legend." Ford's main weakness as a director – his refusal to come to terms with the modern world – pales beside his achievement as the unsurpassed chronicler of pioneering America. He printed the legend better than anyone.

Above: *Watched by George Bancroft (left) and Louise Platt (right), John Wayne (center) surveys the surroundings for signs of Indians in John Ford's classic western,* **Stagecoach** *(1939).*

Center right: *John Ford.*

Top right: *John Wayne in* **Rio Grande** *(1950), the final part of Ford's cavalry trilogy.*

Far right: *Ford (left) directs Dorothy Lamour (squatting, right) in one of his most unusual projects,* **The Hurricane** *(1937).*

Howard Hawks (1896-1977)

Howard Hawks was the most unpretentious of great directors. He sought neither to dazzle nor to moralize. His rule was to tell a story as simply as possible with the camera at eye level. His test was not whether it was profound but whether it was fun.

Hawks' ease within the Hollywood studio system resulted in some of the best films of the traditional genres – the gangster film *Scarface* (1932), the comedy *Bringing Up Baby* (1938), the thriller *The Big Sleep* (1946), the Western *Rio Bravo* (1959). The most original

thing about his work was neither style nor subject, but tone. He makes a joke out of amputation in *The Big Sky* (1952), and puts Cary Grant in a dress in *I Was a Male War Bride* (1949). His adventure films are leisurely, droll dramas of danger, while his comedies are dark and frenzied studies of human embarrassment or uninhibited anarchy. He had a tremendous capacity for making dialogue move, as in *His Girl Friday* (1940), where the fast pace gives the impression of pushy people stepping on each other's lives.

Feminist praise

Hawks' best films convey a kind of team spirit. They are often about a group of professionals collaborating on a testing job, pulling together in the face of danger, each dependent on and confident in the others' ability. Although such films as *Only Angels Have Wings* (1939) and *Red River* (1948) explores the tensions and camaraderie of the all-male group, Hawks also allowed space in his films for strong female roles. Katharine Hepburn in *Bringing Up Baby*, Lauren Bacall in

To Have and Have Not (1944) and Angie Dickinson in *Rio Bravo* are neither sentimental home-builders nor romantic decoration. They are vibrant characters in their own right, often upstaging the men through their insistence on recognition and equality. For this, Hawks has been one of the few classic Hollywood directors to have been applauded by feminist film critics, who see him as a progressive on sexual matters. This was probably quite unconscious on Hawks's part. Characteristically, he was just having "fun" with sexual stereotypes.

Because of the sustained sanity and stability of his world, Hawks remains one of the most pleasurable of filmmakers, relaxed but not indulgent. When he is working at full aesthetic pressure, you see it in the absence of surface strain. He does not need to prove he knows what he is doing: he just knows it, which is satisfaction enough.

Alfred Hitchcock (1899 - 1980)

Above: *Alfred Hitchcock admires himself.*

Alfred Hitchcock made murder into an art form. His thrillers are the most profound and widely imitated in films, not only because of the ingenuity of the plotting but because of his remarkable understanding of violent passion. Hitchcock revelled in the label of "Master of Suspense", but he was master of much more than that.

Hitchcock came to Hollywood in 1939 after a string of slick, scintillating thrillers made in Britain, including *The Thirty-Nine Steps* (1935) and *The Lady Vanishes* (1938). He was slow to get into his stride in his first decade in Hollywood, but there are highlights:

the ever popular romance-mystery *Rebecca* (1940); a subversive thriller about a murderer hiding out in small-town America in *Shadow of a Doubt* (1943); and a spy drama, *Notorious* (1946), which is actually a profound study of trust and treachery in male-female relationships. From *Strangers on a Train* in 1951 until *Marnie* in 1964, Hitchcock never made a film that was less than first-rate. *Vertigo* (1958), *Psycho* (1960) and *The Birds* (1963) are masterpieces.

Technical Hitch

Hitchcock would not talk about his films on a thematic level, preferring to reveal the methods by which he created fear in an audience. He was certainly a technical master, experimenting with ten-minute takes in *Rope* (1948), and with a simple but stunning montage of seeing and reacting that constitutes the entire action of *Rear Window* (1954). But the peerless technique always seemed a means to an end more than the end itself. It locked us into Hitch- cock's world of dark psychosis and dual identity. The mask of our genial host sometimes slips to reveal a romantic anguish and an almost religious obsession with guilt and punishment. *Vertigo* might not make sense as a thriller, but it is one of the most unusual and mesmerizing love stories in movies.

Hitchcock liked to place his scenes of greatest danger in settings of the utmost ordinariness: hence the bi-plane coming out of a blue sky to spray bullets at Cary Grant in *North by Northwest* (1959); the shatteringly abrupt murder in the shower in *Psycho*; and the birds invading the home in *The Birds*. These moments show Hitchcock's gift for the suspense set-piece, his mischievous relish in surprising an audience. They are among the cinema's most startling dramatizations of the eruptions of chaos into a world of order. Hitchcock was a joker of genius, but lurking behind that famous benign profile was also a nihilist, a Catholic moralist, a Freudian sexual psychologist, and an artist whose sensibilities were acutely attuned to our modern age of anxiety. He was a much greater director than he thought, which, given the size of his ego, is an extraordinary thing to say.

Below: *Anthony Perkins discovers something nasty in the shower in* **Psycho** *(1960).*

Below right: *The secret of the cellar in* **Psycho**.

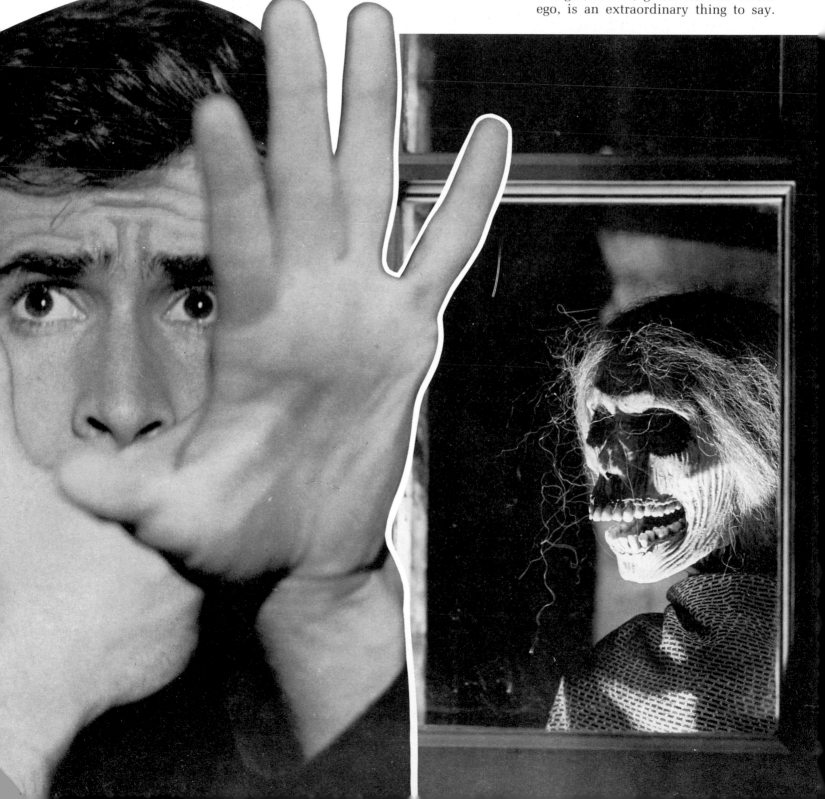

John Huston (1906 -)

Above: *Huston behind the camera on his first musical,* Annie *(1981).*

Right: *Humphrey Bogart and Katharine Hepburn struggle to clear a way through the reeds for their boat in a dramatic scene from* The African Queen *(1951).*

Inset: *John Huston discusses a scene from* Under the Volcano *(1984) with Albert Finney in his Oscar-nominated role as the drunken British diplomat in Mexico.*

"Ah, but a man's reach should exceed his grasp,
Or what's a heaven for?"
So said the poet Robert Browning. In a way, this is the main theme of John Huston's films. Not that they are about Heaven in any orthodox religious sense: his film *The Bible – In the Beginning* (1966) is more interesting on animals than humans, and he has great fun in *The African Queen* (1951) in sticking a spiritual spinster (Katharine Hepburn) next to an irreverent rogue (Humphrey Bogart) and watching the sparks fly. But Huston is intrigued by overreachers, those eccentric, larger-than-life figures like Sydney Greenstreet in *The Maltese Falcon* (1941) or Gregory Peck in *Moby Dick* (1956) who pursue their dreams to the point of self-destruction. Even when their obsessions blow up in their faces, as happens to Humphrey Bogart's gold-prospector in *The Treasure of the Sierra Madre* (1948) or Sean Connery's soldier

of fortune in *The Man Who Would Be King* (1975), Huston is impressed by the grandeur of human aspiration, by the ironies of courage and cowardice, by the stirring way humanity challenges its fate.

Journeys of the mind
Like Howard Hawks, Huston is an adventurer. But unlike Hawks, he is also a psychologist. For Hawks, the point of the adventure is the successful completion of the job. For Huston, it is the revelation of character. He was a good choice to make a film about Freud. His films are psychological quests, dealing with people whose basic motivations are obscure even to themselves.

In his youth Huston had an ambition to be an author and he began as a writer in Hollywood. During his career, he has worked with important literary figures like Arthur Miller, Tennessee Williams and Ray Bradbury and adapted classic

authors like Herman Melville and Rudyard Kipling. His films show a real sensitivity to their literary source, and he often seeks an appropriate photographic style to match the spirit of the original, like the emulation of Civil War photographs for *The Red Badge of Courage* (1951) or of the color of whaling prints in *Moby Dick*.

Nevertheless, however hard he tries to subordinate his personality to that of the material, somehow the wry, wrinkled presence of John Huston always shines through. One feels oneself in the company of a man who spins a good yarn and who is endlessly curious about the more mysterious pockets of human behavior. Maybe this is the reason that many of his films – and not necessarily the most famous – get better and better on reacquaintance. We come to know the man.

Elia Kazan (1909 -)

Elia Kazan's cinema is a melting-pot of Marx and Freud, melodrama and the Method. Born in Istanbul, he emigrated to America with his parents at the age of four. His films are tense, overwrought immersions in the American experience.

During the forties, Kazan's films consisted of sincere, conventional explorations of social problems. He won an Oscar for his indictment of anti-Semitism in *Gentleman's Agreement*

(1947). His theater work during the same period was more adventurous for, as well as directing major new plays by Arthur Miller and Tennessee Williams, Kazan founded the Actors Studio with Lee Strasberg and subsequently brought the Method style of acting into the American cinema. The styles of Actors Studio graduates like Marlon Brando and Montgomery Clift were to influence screen acting for more than a decade.

Sexual neurosis

Kazan's association on three films with Brando – *A Streetcar Named Desire* (1951), *Viva Zapata!* (1952), and *On the Waterfront* (1954) – was particularly important. *On the Waterfront* won an Oscar for both of them and established a prototype Kazan hero: a rebel, anguished and ambivalent about his personal situation and social responsibilities, but with a tremendous drive to solve his problems as an individual. Through James Dean's performance in *East of Eden* (1955), Kazan caught the confusions and longings of a whole teenage generation, just as in his direction of Natalie Wood in *Splendor in the Grass* (1961) he captured something of their sexual neurosis in a materialistic, puritanical America. Both films were

set in the past, yet both seemed to have enormous contemporary relevance.

Like a number of directors of his generation, Kazan seemed to lose contact with mass audiences during the sixties. *America, America* (1964) and *The Arrangement* (1969) were private, semi-autobiographical works, both based on Kazan's own novels. The former deals with the meaning of America for an immigrant looking for a new start; the latter reveals some of the splinters that appear in the typical American success story. Both seem more like intimate diaries than commercial projects, tormented but liberating love-letters to the country of his adoption.

Kazan directs a film with his nerves, holding nothing back. He can be tender and restrained – the lyrical *Wild River* (1960) proves that – but a Kazan film is more typically a thrilling plunge into psycho-sexual whirlpools, with the actors sweeping away an audience in a torrent of emotion.

Left: *Elia Kazan at work on his film version of his own novel,* The Arrangement *(1969).*

Above: *Kazan relaxes between takes with Jeanne Moreau (left) and Robert De Niro (center) on the set of* The Last Tycoon *(1976), Kazan's film version of F. Scott Fitzgerald's novel.*

Right: *Natalie Wood plays a repressed teenager on the verge of a nervous breakdown in* Splendor in the Grass *(1961).*

Above: *A typically ornate Lubitsch set, as the master prepares to direct a scene from* **The Merry Widow** *(1934).*

Center: *Having outwitted the Nazis, the theatrical troupe arrives in triumph in England. One of the final moments of* **To Be or Not to Be** *(1942) with Jack Benny, Carole Lombard and Robert Stack.*

Ernst Lubitsch (1892 - 1947)

Ernst Lubitsch had a style that has been much imitated but never duplicated. Admirers called it "the Lubitsch touch". It was a style of sophisticated comedy in which wit was signalled by a twinkle rather than a nudge, and romantic affairs were conducted with a sardonic slyness that is risqué without being rude. One of Lubitsch's greatest admirers, Billy Wilder, said: "Lubitsch could do more with a closed door than most modern directors can do with an entire bedroom."

Comedies of manners

Born in Berlin, Lubitsch worked as a director in the German silent cinema before coming to America in 1921. He maintained the style of a cultivated cosmopolitan. His plots invariably concern the amorous and financial intrigues of gentlemen and ladies in the more prosperous niches of European society. Through these intrigues, Lubitsch satirized pretension and the insensitivity that sometimes goes with wealth and position. But it was always a well-mannered, polished critique. Underneath Lubitsch's humor lurked a basic idealism. He liked human beings: he believed them to be innately rational and civilized.

His two best comedies are *Trouble in Paradise* (1932), which concerns the nefarious activities of two jewel-thieves in Paris and is a deft blend of sexuality and suspense; and *The Shop Around the Corner* (1940), a wonderfully affectionate study of the love, loneliness and friendship shared by a group of shopworkers in Budapest one Christmas. His two most famous comedies are the sparkling *Ninotchka* (1939), in which Greta Garbo laughs, and the satirical *To Be or Not to Be* (1942), in which Jack Benny plays Hamlet. Actually these two films are not only funny: they are fervently anti-Nazi at a time when Lubitsch must have known that the Europe of his youth, which he had evoked so lovingly on screen, was being destroyed forever.

Below left: *Lubitsch recreates wartime Warsaw in* To Be or Not to Be, *perhaps his last great comedy.*

Above: *Joseph L. Mankiewicz directs Laurence Olivier and Michael Caine in the thriller* Sleuth *(1972).*

Joseph L. Mankiewicz (1909-)

Joseph L. Mankiewicz is a prince of prose. To those who find his films too wordy, he says: "There can never be an excess of *good* talk." Mankiewicz's talk is not only good, it is among the best in Hollywood cinema.

Following his brother Herman (who co-wrote *Citizen Kane*, 1941) to Hollywood, Mankiewicz began by writing dialogue for such diverse talents as W.C. Fields and Rin-Tin-Tin (an unused screenplay about a dog that hates its master, a familiar Mankiewicz theme). After a spell as producer at MGM, which included classics like Fritz Lang's *Fury* (1936) and George Cukor's *The Philadelphia Story* (1940), he began directing in 1946.

Casting for success

He won his first writing and directing Oscars for an adroit study of manners and morality, *A Letter to Three Wives* (1948), and repeated this success a year later with his masterpiece, *All About Eve* (1950), in which theatrical bitchcraft is dissected with a Wildean wit. Mankiewicz's versatility was demons-

trated by the suave spy drama *Five Fingers* (1952) and a musical, *Guys and Dolls* (1955), which, in Sam Goldwyn's words, had "warmth and charmth". He has also made a brilliant film adaptation of Shakespeare's *Julius Caesar* (1953), with Marlon Brando as an electrifying Antony, and proudly claims that *Sleuth* (1973) is the only film to have its entire cast (that is, Laurence Olivier and Michael Caine) nominated for Oscars.

However, the laborious and mammothly expensive *Cleopatra* (1963) proved a disheartening experience. In *Cleopatra*, Mankiewicz murdered Julius Caesar for the second time in his career. It highlighted his films' interest in conspiracy and back-stabbing people. They also frequently feature generation conflicts, and ghosts from the past who will not stay dead. The past is strongly felt in Mankiewicz: he has directed some of the most compelling flashbacks in movies. If his own greatest triumphs now lie in the past, his dispersal of wisdom through wit is an endearing legacy.

Anthony Mann (1906-1967)

Below: *James Stewart undergoes one of his many gruelling experiences in an Anthony Mann western, this time in The Man from Laramie (1955).*

Bottom left: *Mann prepares a shot for the battle sequences of his epic El Cid (1961), filmed on location in Spain.*

Two of Anthony Mann's most popular films are the musical *The Glenn Miller Story* (1954) and the medieval epic *El Cid* (1961). Although these films seem to have little in common, they are both about pioneers whose achievement and example live on after their death. Mann's films were invariably about large-scale heroes, and were critical as well as celebratory of masculine prowess. This was especially true of an extraordinary series of Westerns he made with James Stewart, which uncovered the neurosis as well as the nobility behind Stewart's screen persona.

Dangerously unstable

In *Winchester '73* (1950), *Bend of the River* (1952) and *The Naked Spur* (1953), Stewart plays an ostensibly upright citizen who is actually dangerously unstable. In each film, Stewart is opposed by a charming but deadly villain, who embodies the hero's fear of becoming what he hates. The struggle is thus a fight with the evil inside himself, and the triumphant ending is a victory for character. In these films, and in *The Far Country* (1954) and *The Man From Laramie* (1955), the hero has to undertake a perilous journey across treacherous landscape, which is also a personal journey towards self-knowledge.

When asked to define his typical Western hero, Mann replied: "He's a man who could kill his own brother." The unholy intensity of Mann's films comes through the savage portrayal of family rivalries. Small wonder he was once planning a Western version of *King Lear*. This intensity is heightened by Mann's response to location. The jagged cliffs and swirling rapids of *The Naked Spur*, the lurid skies and ghost-town setting of *Man of the West* (1958) seem part of the films' emotional as well as physical texture. Although he also made fine thrillers and splendid epics, it is the Mann of the Western that particularly reveals his quality as a director.

Right: *Vincente Minnelli looks through the camera.*

Below: *Minnelli directs Barbra Streisand in one of the period sequences from* **On a Clear Day You Can See Forever** *(1969).*

Vincente Minnelli (1910 -)

The name of Minnelli is synonymous with that of the MGM musical. During its heyday, he made some splendid examples – *Meet Me in St Louis* (1945), *An American in Paris* (1951), *The Band Wagon* (1953) and *Gigi* (1958), for which he won his directing Oscar. Some of the greatest set-pieces of the genre – Judy Garland's "Trolley Song" in *Meet Me in St Louis*, Fred Astaire's melancholy monologue, "I'll Go My Way by Myself" in *The Band Wagon*, the stunning French Impressionist ballet that concludes *An American in Paris* – are Minnelli inspirations.

Powerful Melodramas

Minnelli's association with the musical (reinforced by his marriage to Judy Garland and his being the father of Liza Minnelli) might give a mistaken sense of lightness and frivolity. The musicals have their serious side, as in the eruptions of violence in *Brigadoon* (1954) and the cynical sexual politics of *Gigi*. His comedies, like *Father of the Bride* (1950), have an unusual dramatic intensity. Minnelli has also done some very powerful melodramas, notably *The Cobweb* (1955) and the biopic of Vincent Van Gogh, *Lust for Life* (1956),

where the characters' various neuroses and complexes cannot be contained within "normal" society.

As exemplified by *Lust for Life*, Minnelli's films have frequently centered on the plight of the artist in society. This interest seems part of a belief in the superiority of the world of imagination to that of reality. The escape of his characters into a fantasy world unleashes Minnelli's visual panache and expressive use of color and decor. The tension between fantasy and reality makes for vibrant contrast in a musical like *The Pirate* (1948), but is treated tragically in his version of *Madame Bovary* (1949), where the disparity between the heroine's romantic fantasies and the ugly world in which she lives finally destroys her. In indulging his imagination so successfully in the Hollywood Dream Factory, Minnelli might well have fulfilled a fantasy of his own.

Above: "Quiet, please" on a Josef von Sternberg set.

Left: Sternberg relaxes with cultivated Prussian hauteur.

Josef von Sternberg (1894 - 1969)

"An actor is there to fulfil the desire of the director," said Josef Sternberg (whose "von" was the invention of a publicity-conscious producer). His association with Marlene Dietrich through seven films is remarkable evidence of Sternberg's thesis. Every costume, every gesture of the actress seems absolutely under the control of the director.

Victim or temptress

Although he did occasionally adapt literary classics for the screen, Sternberg was never interested in narrative. He thought of himself as a poet. His films are astounding essays on the infinite varieties of love, in which the love-object, Dietrich, is alternately the exploited victim or the tyrannical temptress. In *The Scarlet Empress* (1934) she moves from innocence to experience and from timid grooming to ruthless superpower: it seems as much about Dietrich herself as about Catherine the Great. In their first film together, *The Blue Angel* (1930), Sternberg had shown the degradation of a professor through his obsessive love for a night-club singer. Their last film together, *The Devil Is a Woman* (1935), shows a similar process except that, in this case, the humiliated lover (Lionel Atwill) bears an uncanny physical resemblance to Sternberg himself.

Whatever their autobiographical im-plications, Sternberg's films contain bold insights into obsessive sexual relationships. Their visualization is extraordinary. Sternberg called his style "the play of light and shade", in which smoke, rain, snow, fog, dust and steam are used, in his words, "to emotionalize dead space". Russia, China, Spain and North Africa are evoked without the films leaving Paramount Studios, for these are emotional not geographical locations where shadows and veils correspond to shadings of mood. Sternberg never created real worlds: they are sound-stages of dream and desire in which characters confront their fate. Needless to say – like Dietrich in high-heels following her lover into the desert in *Morocco* (1930), or applying make-up before facing a firing squad in *Dishonored* (1931) – they confront it with style.

George Stevens (1904-1975)

George Stevens' career is a slow dissolve from a master of comedy to a poet of sentiment. He learned his craft as a cameraman on Laurel and Hardy shorts, but attained artistic maturity when America emerged from World War II to Cold War.

His thirties films display a style of humor that is slow-burning and erotic. They include *Alice Adams* (1935), a romantic comedy of class and ambition whose themes anticipate the serious Stevens to come; an elegant Fred Astaire-Ginger Rogers musical, *Swing Time* (1936); and the most rumbustious of Hollywood adventures, *Gunga Din* (1939). The thread of laughter continues into the following decade with *Woman of the Year* (1942), *Talk of the Town* (1942) and *The More the Merrier* (1943), classy comedies with a strong sense of character and an offbeat handling of romance.

Stevens' war experience, which included being part of the American force that liberated Dachau, changed his sensibility. Comedy receded and his films now became full of a feeling of tragic sacrifice, untimely death. *The Diary of Anne Frank* (1959) is his memorial to the war dead.

Stevens' gifts included a knack for directing children, a commanding style, and the ability to make stars act. His films show a rare sensitivity to the yearnings of social outsiders. His key achievement is the trilogy that constitutes his epic reassessment of the American Dream. *A Place in the Sun* (1951) and *Giant* (1956) won him directing Oscars, the former a luxurious tragedy of social and sexual desire, the latter about the transportation of the American frontier spirit into the capitalist ethic. The greatest film of the three is *Shane* (1953), in which the noblest of heroes saves a society that ultimately has no room for him. Stevens' own romanticism had to adjust to a harsh modern world, but it did so with enormous dignity and intelligence.

Top: *The cast of Stevens' World War II drama,* **The Diary of Anne Frank** *(1959). Millie Perkins (seated) plays Anne Frank.*

Above: *James Dean as the cowboy Jett Rink, before striking oil, in Stevens' saga,* **Giant** *(1956).*

Right: *Orson Welles lines up a shot with his cameraman, Gregg Toland, on the set of* Citizen Kane *(1941).*

Bottom right: *Welles' bulky frame (left) exudes corruption in* Touch of Evil *(1958). Akim Tamiroff (right) is about to be killed; a drugged Janet Leigh lies helpless.*

Right: *Welles (left) and Joseph Cotten (right) stand amongst copies of Kane's newspaper, "The Inquirer", in* Citizen Kane.

Orson Welles (1915 -)

"It's the greatest electric train set a boy ever had to play with," said Orson Welles, entering a film studio for the first time. He had been invited to Hollywood on the strength of his sensational theater work and a radio production of *The War of the Worlds*, which had persuaded half of America of an imminent Martian invasion. Given complete freedom by RKO (the last time in his career this happened), he co-wrote, starred in and directed *Citizen Kane* (1941), the greatest directing debut in film history.

Citizen Kane has been seen as a work of prophetic autobiography. The hero is a man of infinite promise who peaks in his youth, his life thereafter being a series of frustrations and disappoint-

ments. But it would be simplistic to interpret Welles' career like that. *Citizen Kane* remains his greatest film but, as *The Magnificent Ambersons* (1942), *Touch of Evil* (1958) and *Chimes at Midnight/Falstaff* (1966) demonstrate, it is not his only great film.

Awesome Welles

The hallmark of Welles' style is virtuosity. The deep-focus effects of *Citizen Kane*, the funfair finale in *The Lady From Shanghai* (1948), the astounding single-take opening of *Touch of Evil* are examples of Welles' technical wizardry. But it is not style for style's sake. It reflects a vision of the world, which Welles describes as "that sense of vertigo, uncertainty, lack of stability, that

mélange of movement and tension that is our universe."

There are two main types in Welles' films: the innocent who has his eyes opened to the guilty world around him; and the egomaniac who wants to dominate that world. As actor, Welles plays the second type, so that his performances of Kane, Macbeth (in his 1948 film version), and the police chief in *Touch of Evil* reveal tyrants corrupted absolutely by power. But Welles the director identifies with the innocents. The bright bravura of his films shows he has retained a youthful enthusiasm for cinema, and for life.

Billy Wilder (1906 -)

"It is not important that a director knows how to write," said Billy Wilder, "but it is important that he knows how to read." Fleeing from Nazi Europe in the thirties and finding work as a screenwriter for Paramount Studios, Wilder became a director principally to protect his own scripts. They are eminently worth protecting.

Wilder made his reputation as Hollywood's resident cynic. He tore into controversial subject-matter such as alcoholism in *The Lost Weekend* (1945) and office politics (professional and sexual) in *The Apartment* (1960), both films winning him writing and directing Oscars. The public liked the Wilder side of life because he could make it funny as well as truthful. *Some Like It Hot* (1959) daringly puts Jack Lemmon and Tony Curtis into drag and a harshly reconstructed St Valentine's Day Massacre into a comedy, and the risk pays off through the sheer pace and outrageous logic of the film's invention.

Wilder's comedy often gains its edge from its counterpoint between farcical content and violent context, the frantic foragings of the heroes of *Stalag 17* (1953) and *One, Two, Three* (1961) taking place against a background of, respectively, a prisoner-of-war camp and Cold War Berlin.

Wilder's moral universe

Wilder brings panache and audacity back into commercial cinema, but there is more to him than sheer cheek. Behind the energy of American enterprise, he shows the dangers of a coldly competitive society where materialism can overwhelm values. He is a humorist but he is also a moralist. Heroes like William Holden in *Sunset Boulevard* (1950) or Kirk Douglas in *Ace in the Hole* (1951) are ambitious social climbers who have a change of heart which, although belated, asserts Wilder's belief in the redemption of character. He is not as cynical as he seems. One

recurrent strategy is to show the melting of American materialism by a confrontation with European romanticism, which mellows Bogart in *Sabrina* (1954) and transforms Jack Lemmon in *Avanti!* (1972), a tribute to Lubitsch that surpasses the Master himself.

In Wilder's majestic Hollywood elegy, *Fedora* (1978), an embittered independent producer (William Holden) complains that "the kids with beards have taken over. They don't need scripts – just give them a handheld camera and a zoom lens." Wilder himself should not be identified with that outburst, for he has been fulsome in his praise for bearded directors in modern Hollywood. Nevertheless, his distinctive care for structure, verbal wit and character development has become unfashionable in a more raucous, ramshackle comedy era. This is the cinema's loss, not Wilder's, for his contribution to Hollywood comedy towers above anything produced in the last decade, and makes his faltering productivity in recent years all the sadder. He would be entitled to endorse the ringing assertion of Gloria Swanson's neglected but still magnificent screen goddess in *Sunset Boulevard*: "I *am* big – it's the pictures that got small."

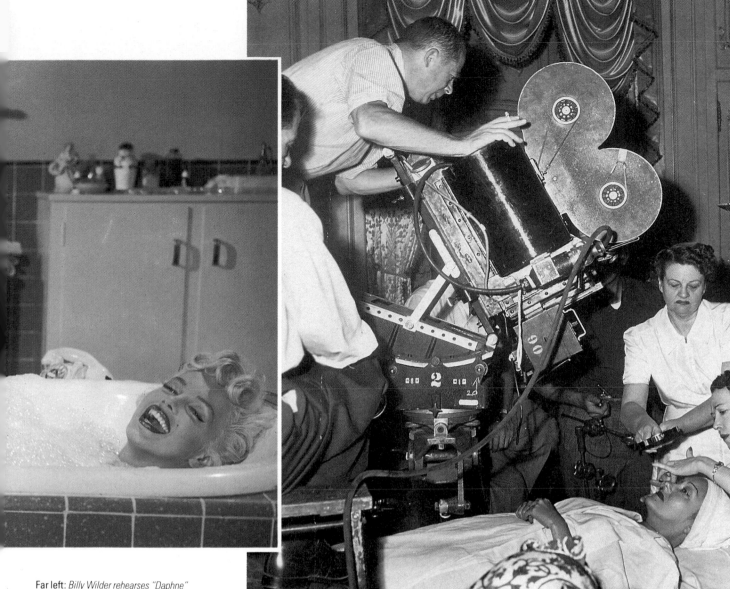

Far left: Billy Wilder rehearses "Daphne" (Jack Lemmon) in the tango sequence from Some Like It Hot *(1959).*

Above: Marilyn Monroe in a glamorous publicity shot for her role in Wilder's The Seven Year Itch *(1955).*

Top right: Wilder directs a scene from Sunset Boulevard *(1950), as an ageing movie queen (Gloria Swanson) undergoes gruelling beauty treatment in preparation for her screen comeback.*

Right: Wilder lines up Irma's poodle for her favorite drink in a café scene from Irma La Douce *(1963). Jack Lemmon and Shirley MacLaine (as Irma) look on in interest.*

Domestic terror

Wyler fussed over the performances because they were the focus of his films. Although he could handle an epic canvas as well as anyone, as the visually resplendent *The Big Country* (1958) and the emotionally overwhelming *Ben-Hur* testify, his forte was for drama in a confined setting. Nobody could make more expressive use of a room or staircase to suggest the struggle for territorial advantage in a marriage or family. Nobody was better at isolating those tiny, cumulative cruelties that can destroy a person's soul. *The Letter* (1940), *The Little Foxes* (1941), *The Heiress* (1949) and *Carrie* (1952) are masterly cinematic studies of terrifying domestic claustrophobia.

Perhaps because of his European background (he was born in Alsace before coming to Hollywood in the twenties), Wyler's subject-matter and approach were always a little off the beaten track. His heroes, like those of *Friendly Persuasion* (1956) or *The Big Country*, tended to be contemplative figures who needed to be convinced of the necessity for action. By contrast, his heroines were often dynamic creatures, kicking against the constraints of a masculine world. Bette Davis has her finest moments on film under Wyler's direction: flaming defiance in a red dress and acting contrition in white in *Jezebel* (1938); ruthlessly refusing to move or be moved during her husband's fatal heart-attack on the stairs in *The Little Foxes*.

Although recurrent patterns and themes are discernible in Wyler's films (unrequited love, class confrontations between the complacent and the envious), Wyler never proposed his work as an expression of his own ego. The cinema, he thought, was simply a place for interesting stories, vividly enacted by a hand-picked, hen-pecked cast. In his supremely gifted hands popular film acquired the passion of the theater and the psychological depth of the novel.

William Wyler (1902-1981)

"They might hate me on the set," said William Wyler, "but they'll love me at the premiere." He was referring to his famed insistence on numerous takes during a film's shooting and the extraordinary results he achieved through such tough tactics with actors. As well as winning three Oscars for himself (for *Mrs Miniver* in 1942, *The Best Years of Our Lives* in 1946 and *Ben-Hur* in 1959), he elicited more than a dozen Oscar-winning performances from his casts. Bette Davis and Laurence Olivier called him a genius. Charlton Heston likened the experience of working with Wyler to "getting the works in a Turkish bath: you damn near drown, but you come out smelling like a rose."

Above: *William Wyler on the set of* **The Collector** *(1965), which won acting prizes for Terence Stamp and Samantha Eggar at the Cannes Film Festival.*

Above right: *Ben-Hur (Charlton Heston, with the white horses) and Messala (Stephen Boyd) are neck-and-neck on the last lap of the chariot race in* **Ben-Hur** *(1959).*

Right: *Gregory Peck (right) plays an Eastern dude eventually roused to action in Wyler's splendid western,* **The Big Country** *(1958). On the receiving end of Peck's punch is Chuck Connors.*

Fred Zinnemann (1907-)

At one stage of his contract with MGM, Fred Zinnemann agreed to go on suspension without pay rather than direct a film in which he did not believe. The gesture shows Zinnemann's commitment to serious film-making, and anticipates similar stands of principle in many of his main characters.

Born in Vienna, Zinnemann had come to America in 1929 and amassed considerable filmic experience, particularly during a long apprenticeship directing shorts and B-features for MGM. His career really took off with *The Search* (1948), a story of European children orphaned during World War II. It presaged a number of films of his about the impact and aftermath of war. Although he has made films in a lighter vein, such as *Oklahoma!* (1955) and *The Sundowners* (1960), these are lesser achievements and his career generally shows the importance of being earnest.

Lonesome heroes

The fundamental Zinnemann theme is that of individual conscience. His most famous films, *High Noon* (1952), *From Here to Eternity* (1953), *The Nun's Story* (1959) and *A Man for All Seasons* (1966), all have the same basic situation. At considerable personal risk, a character takes a stand against a community or institution that wishes the individual to forget his or her principles and compromise and conform. The triumph of the character is that he or she does not wilt under pressure. The tragedy is that such obstinate courage leads to isolation or death. These are dramas of reaction, not action, and so go against the grain of the extrovert assertiveness of conventional Hollywood cinema. The muted endings also challenge conventional Hollywood optimism.

Nevertheless, the success of the films and Zinnemann's Oscars for *From Here*

Above and top: *Zinnemann during the filming of Julia.*

Top right: *Zinnemann prepares to direct the hospital scene from Julia (1977). The heavily bandaged patient is Vanessa Redgrave, in the title role.*

Right: *Henry VIII and his entourage visit Sir Thomas More in A Man for All Seasons (1966).*

to Eternity and *A Man for All Seasons* show how cleverly he has been able to popularize complex themes. A Zinnemann morality play is an absorbing drama, not a dry lecture.

Artists and

Realism, Italian style

The recognition of a European art cinema as an alternative to the dominant Hollywood cinema really got underway after World War II. An early manifestation of it was the work of the Italian neo-realist directors – for example, Roberto Rossellini's *Rome, Open City* (1945) and Vittorio De Sica's *Shoeshine* (1946) and *The Bicycle Thief* (1948). These works represented the absolute antithesis of Hollywood films. They used non-actors instead of stars, were shot on real locations rather than in the studio, were original scripts rather than literary adaptations, and were rough, journalistic and improvisatory rather than technically smooth and studio-finished.

Above all, these films were about real people rather than heroes. They did not narrate plots: they observed life. Their naked truth restored photographic realism to the cinema and simultaneously reopened the cinema as a forum for social debate about a nation's prob-

The great Hollywood directors achieved their greatness in a very different way to their counterparts abroad. National ideology, as well as personal temperament, largely dictated that directors in America should make extrovert, optimistic films, but this did not prevent European-born Hollywood directors like Fritz Lang, William Wyler, Billy Wilder and Fred Zinnemann from going against the grain very successfully, nor did it prevent native directors like John Ford and Howard Hawks working within the traditions of Hollywood genre and narrative in a very personal, intelligent and idiosyncratic way. Nevertheless, it did mean that films were externally orientated towards the audience rather than internally towards the director. With American films – and this is still mainly true – mass audiences went to the cinema because of the stars. With European cinema – and this is still mainly true – a specialized audience went to the cinema because of the director's reputation.

Right: *One of the founders of the French nouvelle vague, François Truffaut.*

Below: *One of the most highly-regarded of post-war Italian directors, Michelangelo Antonioni.*

Moralists

lems. Such realism was to influence Hollywood for a brief period after the war, until McCarthyism had the effect of branding criticism and pessimism as "UnAmerican". The legacy of neo-realism can still be seen today, especially in the techniques of television and the development of dramatized documentary.

New wave in France
During the late fifties several national cinemas in Europe were reawakened by a "new wave". In France, a group of young critics, including François Truffaut, Jean-Luc Godard and Claude Chabrol, had rampaged against the elderly, literary timidity of much of their national cinema. They then set about making their own films, which came like a breath of fresh air. The French *nouvelle vague* used unconventional shooting methods, free-form editing, new faces, and a wholly new approach to film-making born of the young directors' innocence, enthusiasm, and knowledge and defiance of old film forms. Truffaut's *The 400 Blows* (1959), *Shoot the Piano Player*

(1960) and *Jules and Jim* (1961), Godard's *Breathless* (1961) and Chabrol's *The Cousins* (1959) are some of the revelatory French films of this period.

The *nouvelle vague* was supplemented by some remarkable work from an older generation of filmmakers, for whom this atmosphere acted like a tonic. With *Hiroshima, Mon Amour* (1959) and *Last Year in Marienbad* (1961), Alain Resnais brought the complexity of the French "nouveau roman" into narrative cinema. With such French films attracting worldwide attention, the cinema was no longer considered just an escapist outlet for the masses. It was appealing to a wider, well-educated audience that had previously snobbishly derided cinema as popular nonsense.

Art for art's sake?
The Italian cinema had an equally powerful impact at this time. Federico Fellini's *La Dolce Vita* (1960) had enough erotic decadence and obscure symbolism to satisfy the most eager culture-vulture. He followed it with *8½* (1963), a massive self-portrait and self-

confession that demonstrated once and for all the possibility of expressing oneself in film as personally as a writer does with a pen. Meanwhile Luchino Visconti exploded back into form with his violent family saga *Rocco and His Brothers* (1960). Above all, three films from Michelangelo Antonioni – *L'Avventura/The Adventure* (1960), *La Notte/The Night* (1961) and *Eclisse/The Eclipse* (1962) – seemed to catch the whole intellectual mood of the time.

The angry British
In Britain, new directors turned towards working-class realism and the problems of the "angry young man". The British "new wave" was launched with such films as Jack Clayton's *Room at the Top* (1959), which seemed to American critics to display a sexual frankness altogether lacking in Hollywood product, and Tony Richardson's *Look Back in Anger* (1959).

Below: *Tony Richardson lines up a shot.*

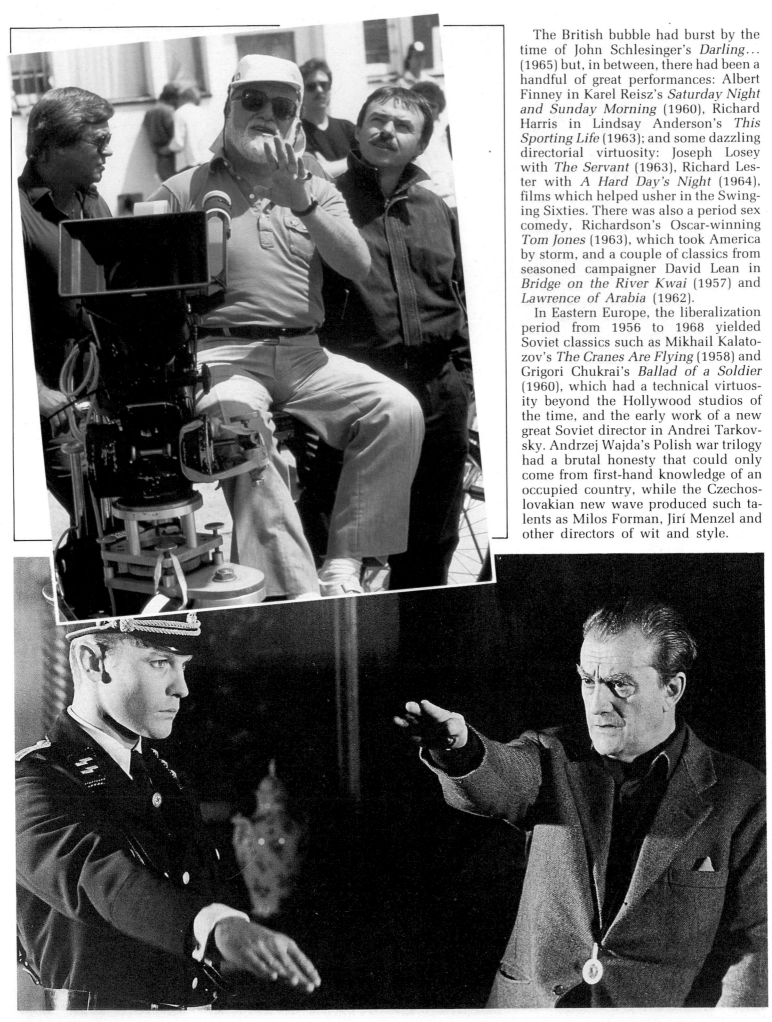

The British bubble had burst by the time of John Schlesinger's *Darling...* (1965) but, in between, there had been a handful of great performances: Albert Finney in Karel Reisz's *Saturday Night and Sunday Morning* (1960), Richard Harris in Lindsay Anderson's *This Sporting Life* (1963); and some dazzling directorial virtuosity: Joseph Losey with *The Servant* (1963), Richard Lester with *A Hard Day's Night* (1964), films which helped usher in the Swinging Sixties. There was also a period sex comedy, Richardson's Oscar-winning *Tom Jones* (1963), which took America by storm, and a couple of classics from seasoned campaigner David Lean in *Bridge on the River Kwai* (1957) and *Lawrence of Arabia* (1962).

In Eastern Europe, the liberalization period from 1956 to 1968 yielded Soviet classics such as Mikhail Kalatozov's *The Cranes Are Flying* (1958) and Grigori Chukrai's *Ballad of a Soldier* (1960), which had a technical virtuosity beyond the Hollywood studios of the time, and the early work of a new great Soviet director in Andrei Tarkovsky. Andrzej Wajda's Polish war trilogy had a brutal honesty that could only come from first-hand knowledge of an occupied country, while the Czechoslovakian new wave produced such talents as Milos Forman, Jiří Menzel and other directors of wit and style.

The last poets?

Not all these directors' films have worn well, and there are many major talents who are hard to categorize, and who represent a poetic strain in the cinema that has not had the attention it deserves. They include Max Ophuls (*Letter From an Unknown Woman*, 1948; *Lola Montès*, 1955); Kenji Mizoguchi (*Ugetsu Monogotari*, 1953); Jean Cocteau (*Beauty and the Beast*, 1945; *Orphée*, 1950); and Michael Powell and Emeric Pressburger (*Stairway to Heaven*, 1946; *Black Narcissus*, 1947).

Nevertheless, the explosion of talent in post-war European and foreign cinema had profound effects, particularly on a new generation of critics who were looking to the new media for a fresh intellectual challenge. The cinema suddenly showed it could handle complex ideas and intricate psychology as well as any modern novel; and that it was possible for an individual creator to make his voice and values heard loud and clear above the cinema's technology, industrial structure and commercial base. Directors from other countries, such as Japan's Akira Kurosawa, Sweden's Ingmar Bergman and India's Satyajit Ray – whose masterpieces were showcased at European film festivals – along with Luis Buñuel, Jean-Luc Godard, Luchino Visconti, Federico Fellini and others were clearly not only among the world's greatest film directors: they were among the century's foremost creative personalities in any medium. Thanks to the contributions of the great directors, by the mid sixties cinema was not just accepted at last as a twentieth-century art form, it was *the* twentieth-century art form.

Top left: *One of the British "new wave" directors of the sixties, John Schlesinger.*

Left: *The aristocrat of Italian cinema, Luchino Visconti, directs Helmut Berger in* **The Damned** *(1969).*

Above: *Jean Cocteau in his last film,* **Testament d'Orphee** *(1960).*

Right: *Jean Cocteau, one of the artist-poets of world cinema.*

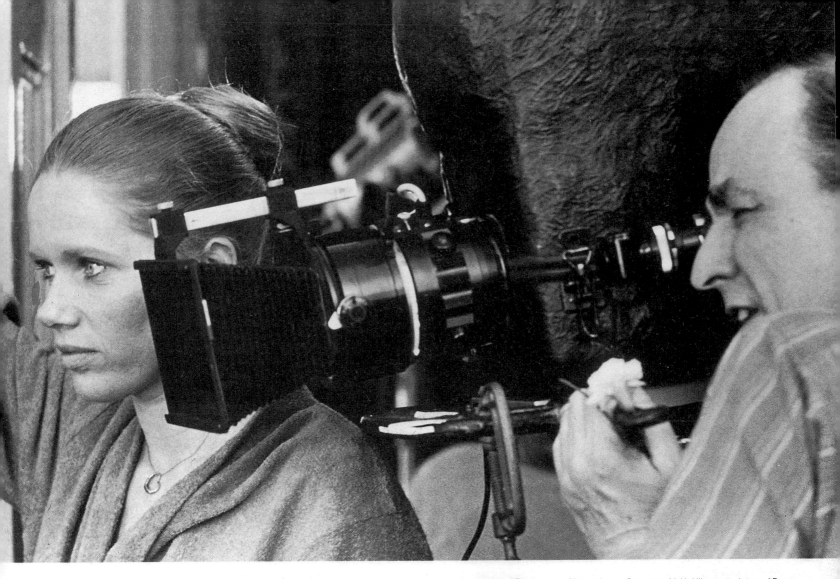

Ingmar Bergman (1918 -)

Above: *Ingmar Bergman with Liv Ullmann on the set of* **Face to Face** *(1976), an intense psychological drama typical of Bergman.*

Right: *A moment from Bergman's study of old age and memory,* **Wild Strawberries** *(1957). Victor Sjöstrom (center) plays the professor who is driven to revalue his past.*

Ingmar Bergman is the definitive example of the film artist. He has always written his own scripts and has gradually assembled a repertory team of performers and technicians who carry out his wishes to the letter. Since he established his international reputation with a trio of masterly works in the fifties – *Smiles of a Summer Night* (1955), *The Seventh Seal* (1956) and *Wild Strawberries* (1957) – he has enjoyed almost complete freedom. For most people, he *is* the Swedish cinema.

To Bergman, the camera eye is the window of the soul. No film-maker's close-ups probe more deeply to the roots of human personality. Films like *The Seventh Seal* and *Winter Light* (1962) particularly test the validity of an individual's religious faith in a world of fearful cruelty. As he developed, he became more concerned with the relevance of art to a modern world either indifferent or hostile to its civilizing influence. At times, he criticizes the artist (implicitly, himself) as a self-centered observer, battening on human misery for his own creative purposes. At other times, he is appalled by the helplessness of the sensitive man in the face of brutal events of recent history, like the rise of Nazism or the Vietnam War. How can a man be a witness to such barbarities and still retain sufficient faith in humanity to function as an artist? Bergman has continued through an astonishing act of will and through a remarkable ability to universalize personal despair.

Triumph in tragedy

There are those who criticize Bergman for the narrowness of his social range, his limited political vision, his spiritual masochism, and even his sloppy dramatic structures with their over-reliance on explanatory narration and misdirected letters. But, in masterpieces like *Persona* (1966) and *The Shame* (1968), Bergman reveals himself as the cinema's most profound tragedian, creating a genuinely cathartic experience out of a confrontation with truth and terror, and summoning awe-inspiring acting from Bibi Andersson and Liv Ullmann. Bergman's stature can perhaps most clearly be seen in the acting he inspires. The kind of self-examination and immersion in a part that typify the performances in his films could only be prompted by direction that imparts extraordinary trust and sensitivity. As a director of actresses, he is incomparable.

The director Arthur Penn put it well: "Bergman's willingness to enter into

Left: Liv Ullmann in a moment of terror from Passion (1969).

what must be enormously painful areas of his life, again and again, in order to understand them and plumb the truth of them, seems to me to be the very essence of the poetic experience." And it should be added that it is not all Nordic gloom. *Fanny and Alexander* (1983), for example, is a stunning reminder of his story-telling gifts, the richness of his visual sense, and his capacity to embrace life with all its pain, perils and pleasures.

Luis Buñuel (1900 - 1983)

There were two main inspirations behind Luis Buñuel's personality and work: atheism and surrealism. His contempt for organized religion ("Thank God I'm an atheist," he said) was revealed in a film like *El/This Strange Passion* (1953), which shows religious orthodoxy as synonymous with emotional repression, or in films like *Nazarin* (1959) and *Viridiana* (1961), which show the impossibility of a modern Christ surviving in today's society. His surrealistic temperament is disclosed in his enthusiasm for symbols and the world of dreams, which subconsciously reveal the hidden fears and violence of modern man.

Buñuel began his career by collaborating with Salvador Dali on a surrealist short, *Un Chien Andalou* (1928), a sequence of unconnected images designed mainly to shock. He then scandalized audiences with *L'Age d'Or/The Golden Age* (1930), an attack on the Church and bourgeois morality (which

Buñuel always found deeply immoral). A documentary exposing the horrific living conditions of peasants in the Las Hurdes area of Northern Spain, *Land Without Bread* (1932), brought this early phase of exuberant anarchy to an abrupt end.

An appetite for satire

After the war Buñuel excelled with a powerful, hallucinatory film about violence and poverty in the Mexican slums, *Los Olvidados/The Young and the Damned* (1950). Films of the fifties like *Adventures of Robinson Crusoe* (1954) and *Evil Eden* (1956) sardonically contrasted man in his civilized and primitive state. With the tremendous international success of *Viridiana* – a blisteringly blasphemous film that amazingly had been made under the noses of the authorities in Franco's Spain – Buñuel embarked on a triumphant final phase. In his later years, he took pleasure not so much in savaging

the bourgeoisie as in, metaphorically speaking, poisoning their food. He served them a dainty cultural dish but there was always a sinister flavor. *Belle de Jour* (1967), *Tristana* (1970), *The Discreet Charm of the Bourgeoisie* (1972), *That Obscure Object of Desire* (1977) all deal with the split between appearance and reality, decorum and desire, and all examine the political and sexual aberrations of the privileged classes with a sly, malevolent eye.

Buñuel's career was a sustained assault on authoritarianism of all kinds. He believed that man was, unconsciously, a slave to custom and to social orthodoxy, and he did everything in his power to shock a spectator out of such unthinking acceptance and to liberate him from blind conformity to Establishment values. His central theme was individual freedom, and his attitude could be summed up in the title of one of his final films, *The Phantom of Liberty* (1974): liberty as a phantom, something intangible, even fearful, always beyond our grasp yet a haunting ideal that must be pursued. The writer Henry Miller succinctly summarized the director's achievement: "They should take Buñuel out and crucify him. He deserves the highest honor that any man can bestow upon another man."

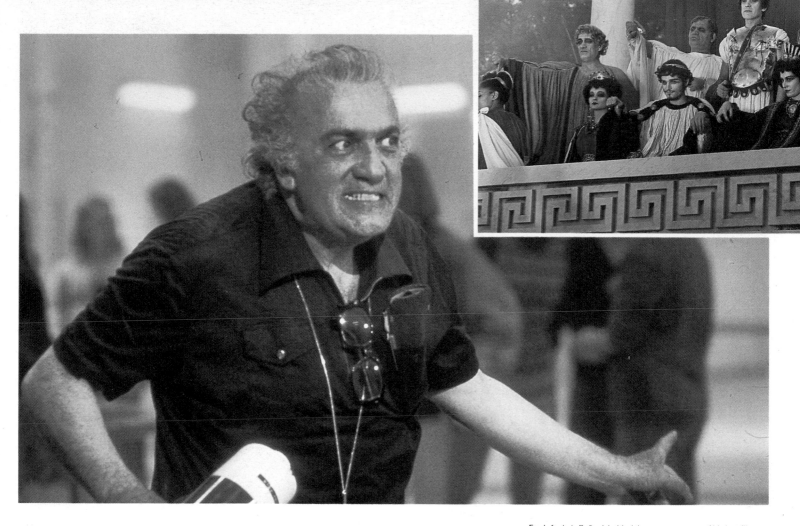

Federico Fellini (1920-)

Frank Capra was proud to have his name above the title, but Federico Fellini has gone one better: he has his name *in* it – *Fellini Satyricon* (1969), *Fellini's Roma* (1972), *Fellini's Casanova* (1976), and so on. He is the director as star, whose work delights in treading a thin line between self-expression and self-indulgence. The films recall Fellini's early experience in the circus and as a cartoonist, being populated by grotesques and having a unique mixture of risk and spectacle, fantasy and fact.

National monument

Fellini is not just a great director: he is a national monument, reflecting the diverse spirit of Italy in cinematic form. He examines sexual values like Michelangelo Antonioni but in a much sunnier, more flamboyant way. He evokes past worlds like Luchino Visconti but with more reference to personal imagination than historical accuracy. His

films have occasionally been dismissed as decadent. *Fellini Satyricon* is certainly that, but the decadence is displayed with such imaginative conviction that George Cukor subsequently thought that "there is only one way I can think of ancient Rome". Depravity in modern Rome is the subject of Fellini's *La Dolce Vita* (1960), but Leonard Bernstein commented: "After three hours of the most abject degeneracy we emerge on wings, from the sheer creativity of it."

Creativity is the key. Fellini's imagination is often comic (as in the magical and mischievous ecclesiastical fashion show in *Fellini's Roma*), and often conveys hidden depths. He rarely just luxuriates in the societies he depicts, but thinks dramatically about how they operate. Far from being a scandalous artist, Fellini might be something of a traditional moralist. *Fellini's Casanova* was no celebration of the life of a rake: rather a sombre

study of a sexual obsessive (splendidly played by Donald Sutherland) whose reputation as lover thwarts his ambitions as politician, philosopher and poet.

The fate of the artist is the theme of Fellini's finest and most famous film, *8½* (1963), in which a film director encounters a creative crisis and ransacks his past for inspiration. On one level a very private, complex and symbolic film, *8½* also succeeds as a universal study of middle-age anxiety and as sheer visual spectacle.

Fellini's work might seem impossibly egocentric, but he has two rare qualities for an egomaniac: the ability to involve a spectator in his world, and a self-deprecating humor. *And the Ship Sails On* (1983) shows him in grand form in the eighties and stars a lovesick rhinoceros that is somehow reminiscent of Fellini himself: thick-skinned, nearly extinct, but still a rare, massive, treasurable creature.

Jean-Luc Godard (1930 -)

To Jean-Luc Godard, we are "the children of Marx and Coca-Cola". In addressing his films to that theme and that contradiction, he became the cinema's chief spokesman for a whole generation of disaffected intellectuals in the late sixties.

Like François Truffaut and Claude Chabrol, Godard was a film critic for the magazine *Cahiers du Cinéma* before he made a sensational directorial debut with *Breathless* (1961). This was a free-wheeling essay on liberty that seemed a curious mating of Albert Camus and *The Big Sleep* (1946) and made an international star of Jean-Paul Belmondo. Godard's early works consisted either of homages to favorite Hollywood films, cinematic love-letters to his wife, actress Anna Karina (notably *Vivre sa Vie* in 1962), or anguished declamations of the transience of love (as in *Le Mépris/Contempt* in 1963) when his marriage began to disintegrate. But the films were becoming more overtly political. *Le Petit Soldat* (1960) and *Les Carabiniers* (1963) were insolent denunciations of war and its degradations, while *Une Femme Mariée/The Married Woman* (1964) was a bold celluloid enquiry into the role and exploitation of women in modern society. One of the themes Godard has insisted on throughout his career has been the idea of capitalism as a form of prostitution, an activity in which people sell themselves, body and soul, for money.

Lost weekend

Weekend (1967) was the turning point. In telling the story of a bourgeois couple whose weekend break leads inexorably to chaos and cannibalism, Godard fashioned his most apocalyptic vision of social and cultural breakdown. Since then, and particularly after the political convulsions of 1968, he has used the cinema as a space not for narrative but for Marxist debate. Star presences like Jane Fonda and Yves Montand (in 1972's *Tout Va Bien*) are merely exploited in order to expose the pathetic sincerity and political timidity of bourgeois liberals (which makes you wonder what Fonda and Montand thought they were doing in the film).

Later films like *Slow Motion* (1980) and *Passion* (1983) are quieter but more disillusioned, the work of an intelligent man now lecturing to convinced disciples rather than potential converts. Godard's films used to throw sparks through their violent confrontations with the present tense. In his revolt against the Hollywood cinema he once

Right: *Jean-Luc Godard inspects footage from one of his films.*

Right: *Violence has spread to the country in* Weekend *(1967), Godard's apocalyptic vision of the collapse of Western civilization.*

Below: *A still from* Tout Va Bien *(1972), one of the films that represents Godard's movement away from "cinema as art" to "cinema as revolutionary politics".*

adored, his hostility to consumerist capitalism of which the cinema is a supreme example, his dislike of an elitist "art cinema" of which he is a principal representative, Godard has become a film-maker without a real base, or purpose. His only route forward would appear to be to render the cinema itself as obsolete. His influence and legacy from those early days can be felt in all spheres of alternative, independent or avant-garde cinema, but his own destiny remains tantalizingly obscure.

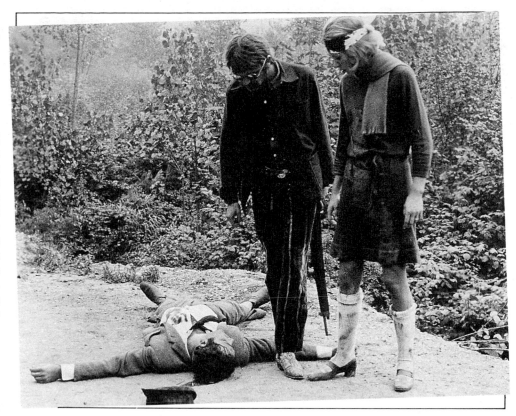

Akira Kurosawa (1910-)

There are not many more exciting sights in the cinema than Akira Kurosawa's direction in full cry. His camerawork conveys a physical sense of movement, particularly when accompanying the massive action of a film like *Kagemusha* (1980). *Seven Samurai* (1954) and *Yojimbo* (1961) are probably the most visually stirring "Westerns" made outside America, which is the reason that they were remade more traditionally as *The Magnificent Seven* (1960) and *A Fistful of Dollars* (1964), respectively. In his Oriental version of *Macbeth*, *The Castle of the Spider's Web* (1957), he solves the old problem of filming

Left: *Akira Kurosawa directs.*

Below: *A typically striking Kurosawa image from **Kagemusha** (1980).*

Above: *The warriors prepare for battle in **Kagemusha**.*

Shakespeare's poetry by ditching it entirely and finding ingenious visual substitutes. In Kurosawa's filmic imagination, the mist-laden forest corresponds to Macbeth's moral confusion, just as the moving of Birnam Wood to Dunsinane visually represents the hero's mental derangement. It is a brilliant example of the cinema's ability to visualize complex psychology.

Camera rhetoric

Psychological extremes have always excited Kurosawa. The style of his films can be generally understood in terms of finding a powerful visual pattern to reflect the feverish inner intensity of his characters. Kurosawa's thematic preoccupation with man's inability to live in harmony with himself and his neighbors is underlined by his restless camera rhetoric.

Like many great tragedians, Kurosawa has a prodigious eye for the absurd.

His masterpiece of truth and illusion, *Rashomon* (1950), collapses boldly into farce as the facts behind the face-saving accounts of a murder come nearer to the surface. *Yojimbo* is a sparkling satire on heroic values, with a corruptible Samurai (Toshiro Mifune) caught in the middle of a struggle between two sides that are equally bad. Films like *To Live* (1952) and *Dersu Uzala* (1976) also disclose a strong humanist vein in Kurosawa, whilst *High and Low* (1963) reveals him as a social critic.

Righting wrongs

For all his association with spectacle (preferably featuring the incomparable Mifune), Kurosawa's work has great variety and compassion. Ironically, his first job with a Japanese film company had come as a result of an essay he had written as a young man called: "What's Wrong with Japanese Movies". For the last 40 years, often against overwhelming odds, Kurosawa has been consistently demonstrating just what is right with Japanese movies.

David Lean (1908 -)

David Lean is one of the great Romantic directors of the British cinema, with an extraordinary sensitivity to nature and a fascination with characters whose cool exterior precariously conceals a passionate temperament. Those critics who see Lean's films as impersonal and blandly middle-class have not really *seen* them at all.

Working his way up from tea-boy to messenger to editor and finally director, David Lean first came to critical and public attention with what were generally regarded as scrupulous, tasteful adaptations of Noël Coward and Charles Dickens. But what emotion Lean brings to Coward's *Brief Encounter* (1945), still unquestionably the British cinema's greatest love story. His version of Dickens' *Great Expectations* (1946) consciously underplays the novel's social criticism and instead emphasizes it as a romantic tragedy, with Pip and Miss Havisham equally savoring the ashen taste of jilted love. *One Woman's Story* (1949), *Madeleine* (1950), *Hobson's Choice* (1954) and *Summertime* (1955) all uncover frustrated romantic yearnings behind the frigid façade of respectable women.

Lean moved into the epic mode with *The Bridge on the River Kwai* (1957), *Lawrence of Arabia* (1962), *Doctor Zhivago* (1965) and *Ryan's Daughter* (1970), but these seemed no less quirkily personal. Beneath a deceptive British reserve, the heroes of *The Bridge on the River Kwai* and *Lawrence of Arabia* were unhinged visionaries, while the heroines of *Doctor Zhivago* and *Ryan's Daughter* pulsated with desire. Such passions in Lean's films often reveal themselves either in emotional reverie, bordering on dream and hallucination, or in a willingness to surrender to the spirit of place. His most recent film is a lively adaptation of E.M. Forster's *A Passage to India* (1984): there could not be a better choice of director for bringing out those erratic, exotic emotions lurking beneath the surface of prim English propriety.

Below: *David Lean in charge of the crew for* **Lawrence of Arabia** *(1962).*

Left: *Robert Mitchum plays a gentle Irish schoolmaster in* **Ryan's Daughter** *(1970).*

Below: *Lean and his crew film one of his most spectacular sequences, the storm in* **Ryan's Daughter**.

Joseph Losey (1909-1984)

Joseph Losey hated the idea of a cinema as a place in which to "kill time" ("as if time were something to be killed!"). For him, entertainment was "anything that is so engrossing, so involves an audience, that their lives for that moment are totally arrested and they are made to think and feel in areas which aren't part of their normal life." His films admirably fulfilled this criterion.

Taking on the philistines

Establishing an early reputation in America for making films that eloquently combined pungent melodrama with a social message, Losey had his career abruptly halted by being black-listed in 1951 during the McCarthyist era. He went to England, working for a while under a pseudonym, and found himself battling with tawdry scripts and philistine producers. *The Sleeping Tiger* (1954) and *Chance Meeting* (1960) are contrived thrillers redeemed by exciting camerawork and perceptive social observation. *These Are the Damned* (1962) is a serious warning of apocalypse that was slipped out in England as a second feature to a Hammer horror film, and the moodily erotic *Eva* (1962) was chopped to pieces by insensitive producers.

His greatest achievement was the trio of films on which he collaborated with writer Harold Pinter – *The Servant* (1963), *Accident* (1967) and *The Go-Between* (1971). Both Losey and Pinter seemed fascinated by the intricate structures and nuances of the English upper class, and spellbound and horrified by the hypocrisies and deceits of its social and sexual attitudes. Pinter's elliptical dialogue was a perfect foil to Losey's precise, suspenseful camerawork, and the two combined to produce three highly acclaimed films.

Losey's later international work combined intelligent and freshly perceived adaptations of classics like Ibsen's *A Doll's House* (1973) and Mozart's *Don Giovanni* (1980) with original insights into some dark areas of modern political life in *The Assassination of Trotsky* (1972) and *Mr Klein* (1976). The films revealed the pessimism of a man who instinctively felt himself an outsider, yet few directors could analyse the absurdities and destructiveness of all varieties of prejudice with a keener intelligence and a more lucid camera eye. With invariably impeccable work from devoted members of Losey's repertory (actors like Dirk Bogarde and Stanley Baker, cameraman Gerry Fisher, designer Richard MacDonald), Losey's films reflected one of the most probing minds in movies.

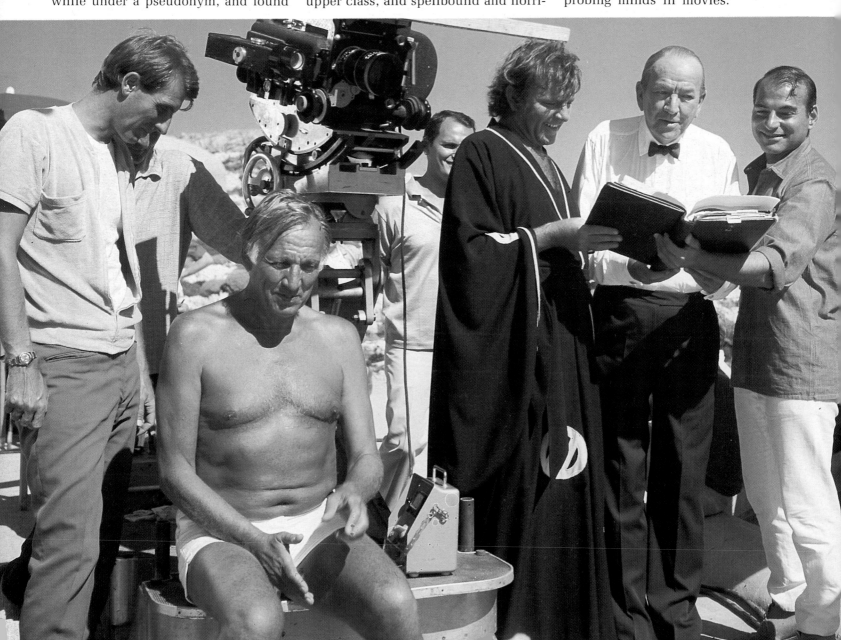

Left: *Joseph Losey (seated) relaxes while Noël Coward and Richard Burton rehearse a scene from* Boom! *(1968), scripted by Tennessee Williams.*

Above: *Losey discusses a moment from* Boom! *with its star, Elizabeth Taylor.*

Right: *Kiri Te Kanawa (right) plays Donna Elvira in Losey's film of Mozart's* Don Giovanni *(1979), which began a vogue for filmed opera and also set new standards for it.*

Satyajit Ray (1921 -)

"In 1950 I went to England and in three months I saw more than ninety films," said Satyajit Ray. "It was *The Bicycle Thief* that finally gave me the idea of how to make my own films. No stars, and mainly on location." His directing debut was *Pather Panchali* (1955), the first part of the *Apu Trilogy*. Since then, the name of Satyajit Ray has become synonymous with quality Indian cinema.

Western impact

Ray's films are rooted in the tradition of humanist documentary, influenced by the social concern of Italian neo-realism, and inspired by the natural lyricism of a director like Jean Renoir. The main subject is India – its customs and culture, its relationship with the British Empire, its conflicts between adherence to a traditional way of life and the impact and influence of westernization. Ray's films have sometimes been criticized for lacking political muscle and for looking too much to the past. But they are about tradition, and Ray's concern for perennial human problems more than issues of national politics is one of the reasons that his films are so accessible to international audiences.

Two major films, *The Chess Players* (1977) and *The Home and the World* (1984), define his position admirably. The former is attentive to the complex politics of turn-of-the-century India, but it places more emphasis on character, beauty, relationships: if only the art of politics had an equivalent sensitivity. The latter contrasts a ruthless revolutionary with a languid liberal, both of whom have right on their side, but again, the subtle shades of human motive attract Ray more than the absolutes of political rhetoric. The films are not sentimental: Ray knows that tragic outcomes can follow the noblest of intentions. But they are optimistic in their continuing faith in people and in their intuitive understanding of the humor and poignancy of the human condition.

Jean Renoir (1894 - 1979)

One of the French cinema's great decades was the thirties and Jean Renoir was its leading light. His use of deep-focus photography anticipated Orson Welles, and his preference for natural locations and a free-flowing camera influenced the directors of the *nouvelle vague* three decades later. Renoir was an innovator by instinct rather than by design. His method evolved simply through a desire to avoid cliché and tell a story as realistically and fluently as possible.

Murder most just

Boudu Saved From Drowning (1932), a comedy about a tramp who runs riot in a bourgeois household, anticipates the theme of class conflict in Renoir that will recur in films like *La Règle du Jeu/The Rules of the Game* (1939) and *Diary of a Chambermaid* (1945). Renoir believed that humanity was divided by class rather than by nationality. On the one hand, this made war an absurdity, a theme Renoir expresses beautifully in *La Grande Illusion* (1937). On the other, it explained Renoir's interest in the manners and mores of different strata of society.

The Crime of Monsieur Lange (1935)

shows the bold relativity of Renoir's morality: in certain circumstances, the murder of a monster can be justified. An exquisite short, *Une Partie de Campagne/A Day in the Country* (1936) harmonizes the rapture of youth with the beauty of nature, until the darkening sky foreshadows the onset of experience. *La Règle du Jeu*, though, is his masterpiece, a film that denounces the moral corruption of French society on the eve of World War II.

Renoir's later films traverse America and India as well as France, and are perhaps less memorable. But his eye for beauty remains comparable to that of his father, the great Impressionist painter Auguste Renoir. His films are faithful to the fundamental precepts of Impressionism, particularly their trust in observation over imagination as the means by which the sensitive individual can come to understand the world.

Below: *Jean Renoir demonstrates the technique of the can-can to his cast. A production shot from* **French Can-Can** *(1955).*

Bottom: *The spectacular can-can sequence that concludes Renoir's* **French Can-Can**.

François Truffaut (1932-1984)

François Truffaut was the man who loved movies. His death in 1984 left all film-lovers feeling as if they had lost a member of the family.

After a career as a notoriously combative critic for the magazine *Cahiers du Cinéma*, Truffaut accepted a chance to direct and made *The 400 Blows*, which won the Best Film Award at Cannes in 1959. As well as being one of the best ever films about childhood, it stunned everyone with its technique – its freeze-frame ending, with the child staring into an uncertain future, has haunted audiences and film-makers ever since. *The 400 Blows* helped launch the *nouvelle vague* and also a series of films, in which the same character, Antoine Doinel, played by the same actor, Jean-Pierre Léaud, grew from callow boyhood to mature manhood.

Truffaut's first film had been part autobiographical, drawing on his own difficult childhood and delinquent adolescence. His concern with children

was to emerge in several movies. *Small Change* (1976) is a study of school life in which childhood is seen both as a state of grace and continuous undercover rebellion. *L'Enfant Sauvage/The Wild Child* (1970) deals with the process by which a primitive, untutored child is gradually educated and assimilated into society: his teacher is played by Truffaut. Indeed, the director himself was an accomplished screen actor, contributing an especially moving performance as the obituary-writer in *The Green Room* (1978), who retains an intense loyalty to his loved ones even after death.

Love and death

Inevitably, Truffaut's films reflect the influence of the directors he loved. *The Bride Wore Black* (1968) and *Mississippi Mermaid* (1969) are homages to Hitchcock, films of dark suspense and (a perennial Truffaut theme) romantic obsession. Through Hitchcock, he said,

he learned how to direct love scenes like murder scenes, and vice versa: love and murder are emotions that are closely akin in Truffaut. His admiration for Renoir was reflected in the glorious *Jules and Jim* (1961), a story of a friendship that not even war and romantic rivalry can sever.

Frequent, rather ominous images of death abound in Truffaut's work: the ending of *Jules and Jim*, with Jules and his daughter carrying the caskets containing the ashes of his dead friends; the death-ridden nightmares in the beautiful *Story of Adèle H.* (1975); the poignant finale of *Fahrenheit 451* (1966) when a dying man recites a favorite book for his grandson to remember. But more typical are the images of life. "Long live cinema!" says François Truffaut's director-hero in *Day for Night* (1973), the most affectionate of all films about film-making. Truffaut's own films will survive as long as cinema itself.

Above: *Jeanne Moreau prepares for bed, watched by Henri Serre, in a scene from* **Jules et Jim** *(1961).*

Right: *Steven Spielberg cast Truffaut in the role of a French scientist in* **Close Encounters of the Third Kind** *(1977).*

Luchino Visconti (1906 - 1976)

Nobody recreated the past more sumptuously on the screen than Luchino Visconti. His sagas about the impact of history and politics on the individual life have left their imprints on such diverse films as Francis Ford Coppola's *The Godfather* (1972) and Bernardo Bertolucci's *1900* (1980), and influential traces of his operatic style can also be felt in the work of directors ranging from Stanley Kubrick and Ken Russell to Tony Palmer and Franco Zeffirelli.

Star transformation

Visconti was a strange mixture of extremes. He was born into one of the most aristocratic families in Italy, but became a committed communist. After a spell as an assistant director to Jean Renoir, he made a number of early films that are classics of Italian realism. However, with *Senso* (1954), he moved from semi-documentary to epic romanticism. His films were aimed at the connoisseur rather than the commercial market, but he liked working with

Above: *Helmut Berger in drag in Visconti's portrait of decadent, pre-war Nazi Germany,* **The Damned** *(1969).*

stars, who often rewarded him with some of their finest work. Burt Lancaster in *The Leopard* (1963) and *Conversation Piece* (1975) and Dirk Bogarde in *The Damned* (1969) and *Death in Venice* (1971) were quite transformed by Visconti's direction.

The films were often studies of forbidden passion – adultery, incest, homosexuality – set against a stunningly observed high society. They seemed at once intimate and colossal, and dramas like *Rocco and his Brothers* (1960), *The Leopard* and *The Damned* are family tragedies on the largest scale. His final films – *Death in Venice, Ludwig* (1973), *Conversation Piece* and *The Innocent* (1976) – are all ambiguous farewells to life. They center on divided, tormented heroes imprisoned by the standards of a society they fundamentally despise, heroically pitting their souls against convention.

Thomas Mann had a phrase for the kind of atmosphere often felt in a Visconti film – "the voluptuousness of doom". Visconti anatomized superficially cultured ways of life in their death throes. At times he pitilessly exposed a deep-rooted sexual decadence (as in *The Damned*); at other times he lamented the slow disappearance of a lofty aristocracy of spirit (as in *The Leopard*). His own death deprived the cinema of one of its most cultured ambassadors.

4 New Voices

All the following directors have established and consolidated their reputations over the last twenty years or so. They have made a sufficiently large and varied body of work to justify an assessment of them as "great". As major film-makers of the modern era, they have absorbed the history and film language of the past. They are developing new forms of expression and are breaking old taboos in their desire to stretch the cinema's visual and thematic range and make films relevant to the audiences of today. Their work exemplifies some of the major changes that have taken place since the sixties.

Sex on the screen

Over the years there has been a gradual liberalization of attitudes about the presentation of sex in films. Europe had led the way. The sex-goddesses of France and Italy in the fifties – Silvana Mangano, Brigitte Bardot, Sophia Loren – had not left a lot to the imagination, and Louis Malle's *The Lovers* (1958) had shown that it was possible to convey the pleasures of physical love on screen without violating artistic taste. The opening hotel bedroom sequence of Alfred Hitchcock's *Psycho* (1960) was something of a milestone in Hollywood sexuality. Directors like Nagisa Oshima (*In the Realm of the Senses*, 1976) and Nicolas Roeg (*Don't Look Now*, 1973) believe in the centrality of sex in human experience, are determined to depict it honestly, but show that it is possible to reconcile visual explicitness with aesthetic judgment and justification. Another important film for the history of sex on the screen was Bernardo Bertolucci's explicit *Last Tango in Paris* (1973).

If Oshima, Roeg and Bertolucci are directors who have pushed back the frontiers of sex on the screen, Arthur Penn and Stanley Kubrick are among those who, in a responsible manner, have explored the limits of screen violence. Penn's *Bonnie and Clyde* (1967) and Kubrick's *A Clockwork Orange* (1971) were both brutally

graphic in their visualization of man's inhumanity to man. But both Penn and Kubrick are film-makers conducting serious enquiries into the causes and effects of violence – rather than simply exploiting it. In a similar way, Sam Peckinpah was to bloody the Western irreparably with *The Wild Bunch* (1969), brutally exposing some of the less savoury legacies of the frontier spirit. Martin Scorsese's *Taxi Driver* (1976) extended these savage bloodbaths into the heart of modern, urban society. The heritage of America's recent history – political assassination, race riots, social protest, Vietnam – suddenly exploded into American cinematic consciousness.

Enter the 'Movie Brats'

Ironically, although the early seventies was a traumatic period in American politics, it was a great period in their cinema. The film capital was temporarily overrun by a group of young, ambitous and talented film-makers with their own way of doing things. Some of them were graduates from film school, which led to their nickname of the "Movie Brats".

Francis Ford Coppola led the way with his magnificently mounted *The Godfather* (1972), and Steven Spielberg followed with a mega-hit, *Jaws* (1975), which, apart from its considerable cinematic achievement, set a whole new style in film selling and advertising.

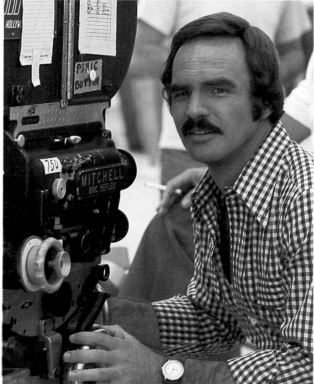

Left: *Maria Schneider and Marlon Brando in the controversial* Last Tango in Paris *(1973).*

Above: *Han Solo (Harrison Ford, right) in George Lucas' mega-hit,* Star Wars *(1977).*

Right: *Burt Reynolds behind the camera, one of the new breed of actor-directors.*

Other talented directors of the new generation like Scorsese, Alan J. Pakula (*Klute*, 1971), Michael Ritchie (*Smile*, 1975) and Brian De Palma (*Carrie*, 1976), were content to make smaller, idiosyncratic, thematically adventurous films that were successful on their own terms.

After the smash hit of *M*A*S*H* (1970), director Robert Altman fashioned a highly individual, iconoclastic path through facets of America's past and Hollywood myths, and his massive collage, *Nashville* (1975) – a wide-ranging essay on the State of the Nation – was one of the most audacious movies of the decade. But, in the period of recuperation after the traumas of Vietnam and Watergate, it was George Lucas's escapist fantasy *Star Wars* (1977) that caught the popular imagination. Its unsophisticated formula of comic-strip adventure, homespun philosophy and technical wizardry blazed a trail that is still being followed as less talented directors than Lucas try to emulate his success.

Within the popular cinema, however, various directors, while occasionally tapping and even initiating successful film trends, have essentially gone their own individual ways. Woody Allen and Richard Lester are two sharp, intelligent talents who have maintained their popularity without diminishing their development. An annual film from Allen or Lester is like a reunion with an old friend.

Nomadic talents

Directors like Roman Polanski and Werner Herzog reveal the cosmopolitan nature of modern film-making. Polanski made his debut feature in Poland, but he is essentially an international director who has proved equally at ease (or ill-at-ease) in Britain, America and France. Sometimes for cinematic reasons (a larger film audience) and sometimes for political reasons (freedom from censorship), other Eastern European directors have taken their cue from Polanski and moved westwards, often with great success. They include the Pole Jerzy Skolimowski (*Moonlighting*, 1982) and the Czech Milos Forman (*One Flew Over the Cuckoo's Nest*, 1975, and *Amadeus*, 1984).

Before he became a cinematic globe-trotter, Werner Herzog was a key figure in another important development of recent film history – the new German cinema of the seventies. These were films that critically reassessed their country's pre-war Nazi past and its post-war economic "miracle". Herzog expressed his contempt for most aspects of modern German society by scrupulously ignoring it in favor of metaphysical rather than contemporary issues. Wim Wenders investigated the impact of American culture on the post-war German generation, only to be seduced by it and wind up in America himself. After a tough apprenticeship on *Hammett* (1982), he hit the jackpot with *Paris, Texas*, the most accessible art movie of 1984. With Herzog and Wenders, the other major figure was Rainer Werner Fassbinder who, before his death in 1982, was to make around

Above: *One of the most popular stars of modern cinema, Jack Nicholson. He won a Best Actor Oscar for* **One Flew Over the Cuckoo's Nest** *(1975).*

Right: *Sir Richard Attenborough is all smiles, having won Best Director and Best Film Oscars for his personal project,* **Gandhi** *(1982).*

Far right: *Steven Spielberg poses with his extra-terrestrial friend. A publicity still from Spielberg's* **E.T: The Extra-Terrestrial** *(1982).*

forty films, nearly all anguished melodramas about social and sexual oppression. Volker Schlöndorff has made a speciality of carefully crafted adaptations of modern literary classics, notably Grass' *The Tin Drum* (1980) and Proust's *Swann in Love* (1984). In the meantime Schlöndorff's wife, Margarethe von Trotta, has established a reputation as one of the world's great woman directors on the basis of films like *The German Sisters* (1981) and *Friends and Husbands* (1983).

Various national cinemas have come into greater prominence in recent years. We are still learning more about the history and development of cinema in Japan, China, India and South America.

The Australian cinema enjoyed a great vogue during the seventies, with three of its major directors – Peter Weir, Bruce Beresford and Fred Schepisi – subsequently making films in America. The British cinema strove to make significant inroads into its home and international markets, encouraged by the world-wide success of Hugh Hudson's *Chariots of Fire* (1981) and Richard Attenborough's *Gandhi* (1982).

Director as superstar

Despite the unpredictability of audiences, it is still possible for directors to make their presence felt. This book began by considering that the cinema of the most famous personality worldwide that the cinema has ever seen, Charles Chaplin. Appropriately, it ends with a look at the most extraordinary directorial phenomenon of the postwar era, Steven Spielberg. At the time when a whole industry's confidence has alternately wavered, declined and almost collapsed, Spielberg has demonstrated more than anyone that worldwide enthusiasm for film is as keen as ever. He is the biggest box-office name in the cinema today. To the categories of director as pioneer, as hired hand, as craftsman, as artist, Spielberg has added a new category for himself: film director as superstar.

Woody Allen (1935 -)

As a performer, Woody Allen became so popular as everyone's favorite failure that his more recent films have had to concentrate on the drawbacks of success. As a director, he has moved from the technical rawness of early comedies like *Take the Money and Run* (1969) and *Bananas* (1971) to a stylistic tour-de-force of which Orson Welles would have been proud, *Zelig* (1983). He has taken risks and sprung a few surprises, so that nowadays a new Woody Allen film is a major event.

There have been three distinct, steadily upmarket progressions so far in Allen's career. He began as a walking worry-head whose incompetence as Castro in *Bananas* and as Casanova in *Play it Again, Sam* (1972), which he wrote but did not direct, seemed to align him with prior American film farceurs like his favorite, Bob Hope. *Love and Death* (1975) was a still amusing but more ambitious revelation of Allen as a jokey intellectual, playing games with cultural classics like *The Seventh Seal* (1957) and *War and Peace*. But with the award-winning *Annie Hall* (1977) and *Manhattan* (1979), he moved into a different gear altogether: still comedy, just, but with a pathos born out of personal experience, and a preference for Manhattan realism rather than Marx Brothers farce. Allen now offered himself not as the endearing comic loser but as a wry, bruised expert on urban anxiety.

Allen's agony

Allen has referred to himself as "a product of TV and psychoanalysis" and under the laughter there is certainly

Left: *Diane Keaton and Woody Allen. Keaton won an Oscar under Allen's direction in* **Annie Hall** *(1977).*

Below: *Woody Allen as the human chameleon and Mia Farrow (left) as his psychiatrist in* **Zelig** *(1983).*

Left: *Woody Allen directs.*

Below: *Diane Keaton and Woody Allen are romantically silhouetted in* **Manhattan** *(1979).*

any amount of neurosis. His straight drama, *Interiors* (1978), is a study of family breakdown that seems closer to Chekhov than Chaplin. The thinly veiled autobiography of *Stardust Memories* (1980) is a scream of pain from someone for whom the American Dream of fame and fortune has led to alienation, not fulfilment. Even amidst the laughter, his films have a monochrome melancholy that derives from a knowledge of what the pursuit of art and ambition can do to relationships.

Among other things, his work is about the search for the Perfect Woman, represented very effectively in a variety of films by Diane Keaton and Mia Farrow. He has it within him to make a great romantic film, or, for that matter, a great anything. "This year I'm a star," he said once, in that unmistakable tremulous tone, "but what about next year – a black hole?" Woody's star will surely endure, even though he once said that he did not wish to achieve immortality through his work – he would prefer to achieve it by not dying.

Francis Ford Coppola (1939 -)

Coppola is the Godfather of modern American cinema. He is confidante and father-figure to that generation of directors like George Lucas and Steven Spielberg who emerged from film school to storm Hollywood in the seventies. A businessman with creative vision, he has financed the work and film distribution of foreign directors like Akira Kurosawa, Werner Herzog and Wim Wenders. In the meantime, his own directing career has taken a strange, unpredictable course.

Coppola made his directing debut on a preposterous horror quickie, *Dementia 13* (1963), ensuring that the absurd plot was buried under the kind of fancy camera-angles that get a young director noticed. His other efforts during the decade veered between the petty (*You're a Big Boy Now* in 1966), the pretty (*Finian's Rainbow* in 1967) and the pretentious (*The Rain People* in 1969). But he was learning the craft, acquiring a mastery of camerawork and montage, and, in *Finian's Rainbow*, showing an instinctive facility for filming musical numbers. His screenwriting expertise won him an Oscar for *Patton* (1970), directed by Franklin Schaffner.

The Godfather (1972) and *The Godfather, Part II* (1974) established him as a modern master. They updated the conventions of the gangster genre, combining the sweep of a dynastic family melodrama with a mature political analysis of corporate America. They restored Marlon Brando to superstardom and justly made stars of the prodigiously gifted Al Pacino and Robert De Niro. Coppola's following film, *The Conversation* (1974), was on a smaller scale but seemed an equally potent fable for the times, about a hermetic surveillance expert (Gene Hackman) who stumbles on a murder plot. The apparatus of treacherous tapes and the atmosphere of paranoia had prophetic echoes of Watergate.

The heart of darkness

Shot on a budget of $31.5 million, *Apocalypse Now* (1979) concluded Coppola's decade in spectacular style. Horrific tales of the shooting had abounded. The budget escalated; actor Martin Sheen suffered a heart attack; Coppola thought he was going mad; and industry cynics were dubbing the seemingly doomed production "Apocalypse When?" But Coppola delivered the goods, a spellbinding metaphysical allegory in which America's incursion into Vietnam is interpreted as a mad journey into the dark heart of man and his capacity for primitive evil.

Top: *Coppola, behind camera, directs.*

Above: *The Godfather with his successor – Marlon Brando hands over the reins to Al Pacino in* **The Godfather** *(1972).*

This production may have taken its toll. Certainly Coppola's films for the eighties – *One From the Heart* (1982), *The Outsiders* (1983), *Rumble Fish* (1983) – have seemed strangely withdrawn, private works on an incongruously grand scale. The seventies had stimulated Coppola's speciality for big American themes: the present decade seems not to have inspired him in the same way. Has the Godfather lost his touch? It would be a complete surprise if so complete a film-maker as Coppola did not once again make audiences an offer they cannot refuse.

Right: *Soldiers and Montagnard tribesmen guard the temple of their "god" Kurtz (Brando) in **Apocalypse Now** (1979).*

Below: *To the accompaniment of Wagner's "Ride of the Valkyries", American helicopters launch an attack on a Vietcong beach-head in **Apocalypse Now**.*

Werner Herzog (1942 -)

"I don't want to live in a world where there are no lions anymore, or no people like lions," says Werner Herzog. He believes that modern society is stuffy and sterile, separating people from their natural instincts. His films do not criticize contemporary life: they attempt to transcend it.

Herzog's films venture where cameras rarely go. The filming of *Aguirre, Wrath of God* (1973) – about a sixteenth-century search for Inca gold – involved a trek across hazardous locations in Peru. In *Fitzcarraldo* (1982), the scheme of the title character (Klaus Kinski) to build an opera house in the middle of the Amazon jungle seems no more insane than Herzog's decision to

film on authentic locations – though at one stage he had to pull a gun on Kinski to force him to continue – and similarly to try to move a large boat across a mountain. "Dreams move mountains," he says: it is his philosophy of film-making.

Visionaries and eccentrics

Herzog has little interest in conventional or "normal" society, other than as something to react against with all possible force. There are only two kinds of people to whom he responds: the visionaries and eccentrics, like Aguirre or Fitzcarraldo; and the neglected, the insulted and injured, those whom normal society rejects. Signifi-

cantly, when Herzog remade the horror classic, *Nosferatu, the Vampyre* (1979), the monster is not unsympathetic – after all, he has no control over what he is. Herzog rather relishes the demonic plague unleashed on the bourgeois community; at last something shocks them out of their smug complacency. In *The Enigma of Kaspar Hauser* (1975), the hero is seen as a freak by society. To Herzog, it is society that is deformed, not Kaspar, who responds to Nature and to experience in a warm, vital, instinctive manner. Kaspar is the most endearing of Herzog's outsiders, and Bruno S. plays him unforgettably.

In making these punishing fables about the discontents of civilization and the rejection of the everyday, Herzog has pushed his actors (notably, the resilient and remarkable Kinski) to astonishing extremes. "People interest me when they are on the point of breaking apart," says Herzog mischievously, "when their cracks become visible…" Extremes of sensation are what Herzog seeks in his work: not analysis, but agitation of the mind. As with all visionaries, the line between madness and sublimity is a thin one, but life is never dull, and neither are their films.

Left: *Klaus Kinski menaces Isabelle Adjani in Herzog's* **Nosferatu, the Vampyre** *(1979), a remake of the German silent horror classic.*

Above: *Werner Herzog advertises* **Fitzcarraldo** *(1982), a prize-winner at the Cannes Film Festival.*

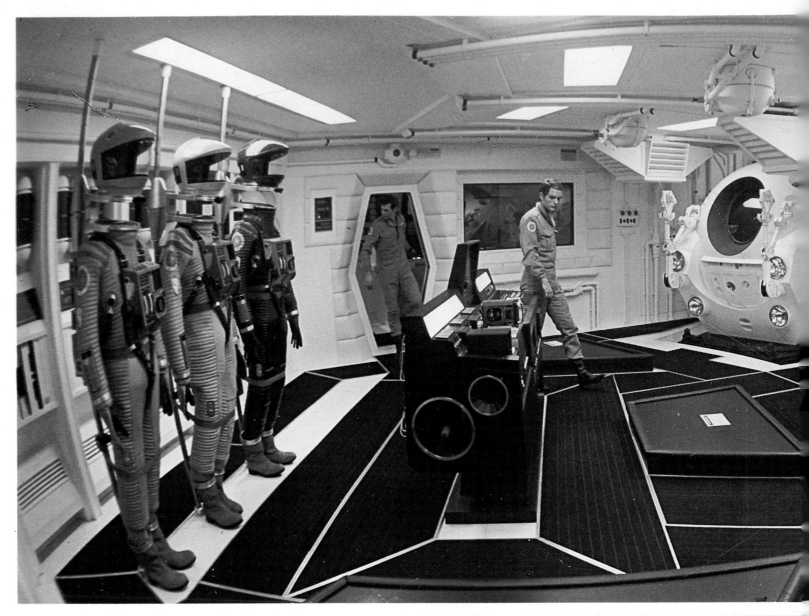

Stanley Kubrick (1928 -)

One of the most stimulating aspects of Stanley Kubrick's career is that no two films of his are quite alike. Nevertheless, all of them are underpinned by a powerful personality with a formidable intellect who has managed to achieve for himself a rare position of independence within the industry.

Kubrick's early films show signs of things to come. *The Killing* (1956) and *Paths of Glory* (1957) are both clinical studies of human fallibility, in which plans devised with clockwork precision – in one case a robbery, in another a military advance during World War I – go disastrously wrong. *Lolita* (1962) and *Dr Strangelove* (1964) reveal Kubrick's mordant black humor, the first a

study of sexual obsession leading to madness and murder, the second a study of military and political insanity leading to global annihilation.

Each Kubrick film seems to take the argument of his previous film a step further. *Dr Strangelove* showed the tension between man and the machine. *2001: A Space Odyssey* (1968) develops this theme into an expansive thesis on man's evolution and the degree by which man has been mastered by the technology he has created. After *2001* came the controversial *A Clockwork Orange* (1971), which debates the issue of free-will through the tale of a teenage hoodlum ostensibly cured of his violence by the application of science.

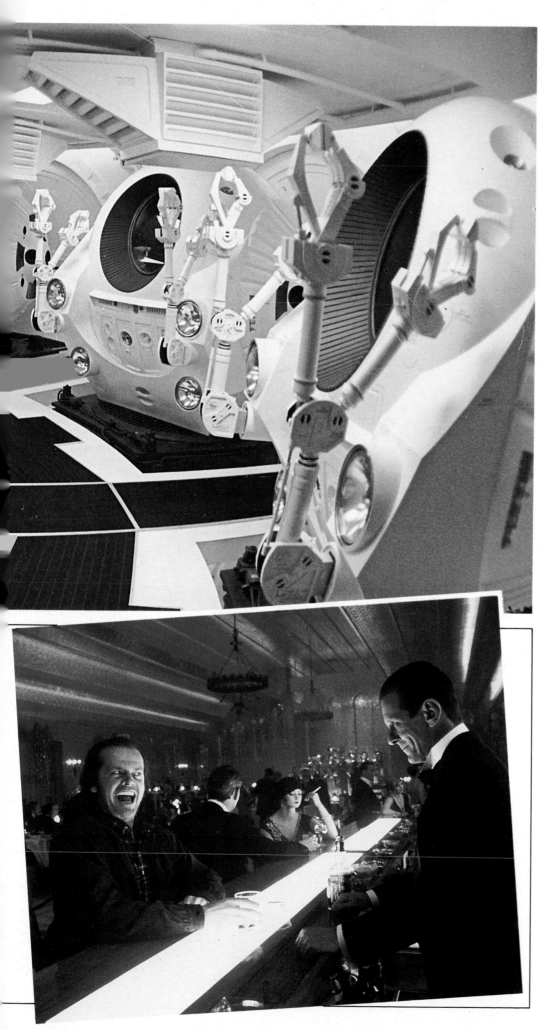

Above: *Stanley Kubrick lines up a scene.*

Left: *A futurist interior from the science-fiction epic,* 2001: A Space Odyssey *(1968).*

Bottom left: *Sue Lyon plays the seductive young heroine of* Lolita *(1962).*

Bottom right: *Jack Nicholson in* The Shining *(1980).*

Rake's progress

In many ways, Kubrick's later films, *Barry Lyndon* (1975) and *The Shining* (1980), have been his most awesome and experimental. *Barry Lyndon* is the cautionary tale of a rake's progress and come-uppance in the high society of the eighteenth century. It has a claustrophobic sense of time, an infinite sense of space, and one of the most stunning visual surfaces of any film. By contrast, *The Shining* is a labyrinthine horror film, in which a frustrated American writer slowly goes mad in an icy haunted house that becomes an image of his mind, reflecting his frozen sensibility and producing Gothic ghosts out of the corridors of his paranoid imagination.

Kubrick's films have tended to focus on heroes who have found it impossible to adapt their spirit to the period in which they live. He is fascinated by the tensions between the individual and history, between man and science, and between language and social conditioning. He has been criticized for two central absences in his films – namely, women and human feeling – but it is likely that he feels that the virtues of both fall outside of his specialized field of study. The societies he analyses are impersonal and masculine, and he approaches and analyses them more in the manner and spirit of a scientist than an artist. For Kubrick, the cinema is a laboratory for observation and experiment. His findings have revealed a mind of the highest intellect and provoked more critical debate than any American director since Orson Welles.

Richard Lester (1932 -)

Because of his direction of the Beatles on *A Hard Day's Night* (1964) and *Help!* (1965) – and no pop personalities have ever been better served on film – Richard Lester was quickly identified with Swinging London and the sixties youth revolution. The identification was confirmed by his award-winning comedy, *The Knack* (1965), whose frisky style seemed inseparable from its social optimism and its exuberant annihilation of the values of an older generation. To some extent, Lester has never entirely shed that image of the "mod" director with the excitable camera. In fact, both time and the times have had their effect.

His disillusionment with the betrayal of sixties idealism yielded a trio of films of unexpected complexity and depth. *How I Won the War* (1967) bitterly mocked bland patriotism and the heroics of war pictures. His masterpiece, *Petulia* (1968), reflected the convulsions of 1968 America through the doomed, violence-crossed romance of an older man and a younger married woman, in a San Francisco whose flower-power "summer of love" is in its death throes. *The Bed Sitting Room*

(1969) was a surrealistic nuclear comedy about a blitzed Britain, in which the survivors – all 23 of them – act out a travesty of bourgeois existence. London was sinking now, now swinging, an eloquent metaphor for the submergence of Lester's hopes for the decade.

Lester's legends

By contrast, the following decade saw Lester concentrating mainly on historical subjects. *Royal Flash* (1975) and *Butch and Sundance – the Early Days* (1979) wittily explored the gap between legend and reality (as had the Beatles films, in their way), while the beautiful *Robin and Marian* (1976) took the same theme to an overwhelmingly emotional, even tragic, conclusion. *The Three Musketeers* (1973) cleverly caught the dark social satire that modifies Dumas's romanticism: the swashbuckling had a real sting to it. The films set in modern times were mainly political thrillers. *Juggernaut* (1974) was one of the best British films of the seventies, a suspenseful, searching examination of the condition of England of 1973-4. The anarchic *Cuba* (1979), set on the eve of Castro's revolution, mixed the emotions of renegades, romantics and revolutionaries like an explosive cocktail. With *Superman II* (1980), Lester soared back into the heart of mainstream cinema.

Lester has often been seen as a sort of cinematic court jester, but his quickwittedness should not be mistaken for frivolity. He has not lost his scepticism about heroes or society, nor the ability to create worlds on screen that crackle with a sense of crisis and excitement. The frequent war games in his films seem to reflect his vision of life itself as an absurdist battle. I cannot think of a film director who has given more sheer pleasure over the last two decades, yet without compromising his intelligence or iconoclasm. Lester's talent is a tonic.

Left: *Richard Lester directs one of his favorite actors, Michael Hordern, who appeared in* How I Won the War *(1967) and* The Bed-Sitting Room *(1969).*

Bottom left: *Christopher Lee plays the villainous Rochefort in* The Three Musketeers *(1973).*

Below: *Christopher Reeve in something of a tangle as he tackles malevolent computers and video games in* Superman III *(1983).*

Nagisa Oshima (1932 -)

A member of the Japanese cinematic generation that succeeded great directors like Akira Kurosawa, Kenji Mizoguchi and Yasujiro Ozu, Nagisa Oshima formulated his ideas during the traumatic period of his country's history after defeat in World War II and, more specifically, after Hiroshima. His early films were particularly concerned with the malaise of post-war Japanese society, the contamination, as he saw it, of westernization, and the political failure of the Left to make a breakthrough.

Oshima came to international attention with three films – *Diary of a Shinjuku Burglar* (1969), *Death by Hanging* (1968) and *Boy* (1969). The style was unconventional in its ritualized theatricality and the shifts between fantasy and reality. Two things were especially noticeable. His main characters were often, in conventional terms, "criminals", but Oshima chose to see them as intriguing misfits whose personalities seemed to deny them a constructive role in modern society: what are the ways in which such characters can express themselves? The second theme, intimately connected with the first, was the emphasis on sexual relationships, a space in which the characters could find personal freedom but which has repressions and pitfalls of its own.

Oshima's most notorious film, *In the Realm of the Senses* (1976), was a logical culmination of this: the story of a couple whose insatiable passion for each other is a (temporary) way of denying the restrictions of the world outside and finding liberation within themselves. *Empire of Passion* (1978) was a sort of sequel, a gloomy ghost story in which a husband who has been murdered by his wife and her lover comes back to haunt them, in the process uncovering their crime. The release of the first film finds its echo in the repression of the second.

Merry Christmas Mr Lawrence (1983) is also about forbidden passion. A Japanese Captain (Ryuichi Sakamoto) becomes fascinated by a prisoner of war (David Bowie), the "enemy" suddenly becoming dangerously attractive rather than alien and contemptible. It is a variation on Oshima's preoccupation with society's "enemies" whose psychology he seeks to understand rather than condemn. What is different in *Merry Christmas Mr Lawrence* is the look towards the west. His previous films have been idiomatic interrogations of Japanese society. The film offers a thematic broadening of scope, and an encouraging trailer for Oshima's future international progress.

Below: *Nagisa Oshima prepares to shoot a scene.*

Right: *The prison hospital in* **Merry Christmas Mr Lawrence** *(1983), Oshima's first big international film.*

Bottom right: *After insulting the Japanese officer, David Bowie is buried alive in* **Merry Christmas Mr Lawrence.**

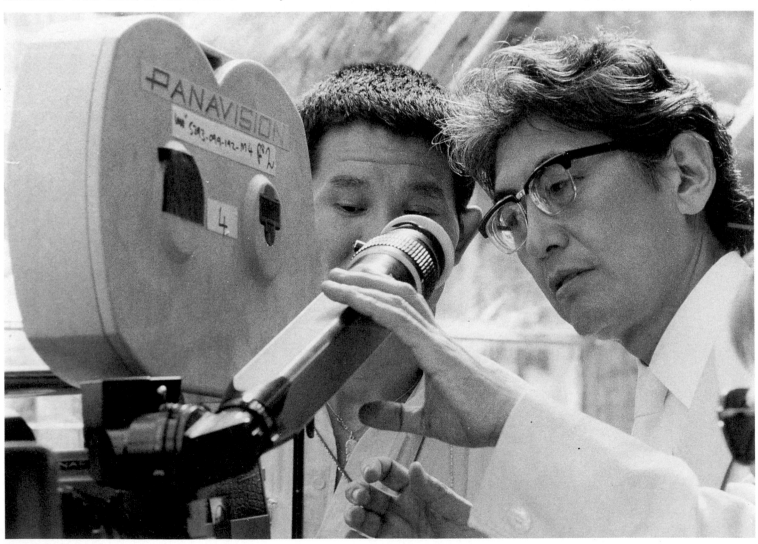

Arthur Penn (1922 -)

Top: *Arthur Penn (center).*

Above: *Warren Beatty as Clyde Barrow is shot during one of many violent scenes in* Bonnie and Clyde *(1967).*

Top right: *A detail from Penn's memorable re-creation of the Battle of the Little Big Horn in* Little Big Man *(1970).*

Right: *Dustin Hoffman stars as the white man brought up by Indians in* Little Big Man.

Arthur Penn is an intelligent director on a difficult mission: to create a counter-culture within mainstream American cinema. Most of his films have been made within the popular genres – gangster (*Bonnie and Clyde*, 1967), mystery thriller (*Night Moves*, 1975) and Western (*The Left-Handed Gun*, 1958; *Little Big Man*, 1970; *The Missouri Breaks*, 1976). But all of them are eccentric in some way, looking at the form from a fresh perspective. Penn romanticizes the American outsider, whether he is a gangster or an Indian, and questions the heroic stature of American prototypes such as the Western hero and the private-eye.

To date, his most successful film has been *Bonnie and Clyde*. Although set in the thirties, it had enormous relevance for the disaffected youth of the sixties, who were in protest against the values

of prophecy of a backlash against sixties "permissiveness" – was disproportionately severe. Later films like *Alice's Restaurant* (1969), *Night Moves* and *Four Friends* (1981) have revisited the sixties in a tone of painful nostalgia, surveying a battlefield of crushed hopes. Punctuating these reflections have been two bleakly comic Westerns, *Little Big Man* and *The Missouri Breaks*, which both expound alternative narratives to those traditionally propounded about the growth of the United States.

Penn's mythic interrogations probably seem a little out of fashion now in an America that is beginning to believe in its myths again. He is now grouped as a sort of partner-in-crime to fellow mavericks like Robert Altman, who shares Penn's irony and cynicism; and is a sort of father-figure to younger directors like Terrence Malick, the maker of *Badlands* (1973) and *Days of Heaven* (1978), whose jagged narrative rhythms, stylized violence and savage pastoralism owe a lot to Penn. An Arthur Penn film is an unsettling experience, but real evidence of a lively filmic mind in action. It does not make you feel better, but it certainly makes you think.

of their elders and experimenting with alternative life-styles. At the time, the film seemed the culmination of a particular direction in Penn's career. It uncovered the reality behind characters who had become legends in their lifetimes, like his film about Billy the Kid, *The Left-Handed Gun*. It went further than Penn's previous film, *The Chase* (1966), in analysing the link between violence and sexual repression in America. *Bonnie and Clyde's* extraordinary leaps between hillbilly comedy and hysterical carnage excited and disturbed contemporary audiences, for whom Penn brought topicality and color – more specifically, blood – back into the traditional gangster film.

Although he did not sentimentalize the violence of Bonnie and Clyde themselves, he certainly suggested that the violence directed against them – a kind

Roman Polanski (1933 -)

"Who's the midget?" asks Jack Nicholson's detective in *Chinatown* (1974), when he is being menaced by a baby-faced psychopath who responds by slashing his nose with a knife. The "midget" is actually the film's director, Roman Polanski.

Polanski's films are rather like this character: king-sized malevolence deceptively contained in a pint pot. They ask impudent questions, and generally come up with terrifying answers. Nearly all are stories of violence and mur-

der, laced with philosophical musings and a grisly humor.

The disquieting tone of the films can be traced directly to Polanski's sensational life. His childhood in war-torn Poland was horrific, his mother dying in a Nazi concentration camp, Polanski himself narrowly escaping death on numerous occasions. In 1969, his wife, actress Sharon Tate, was murdered in California by the Manson "family". In 1977, Polanski was arrested for having intercourse with an under-age teenager,

which led to his imprisonment in America and ultimate exile from that country.

The traumas of such a life have inevitably colored the films. Terror and psychological disturbance dominate the British-made *Repulsion* (1965) and the French-made *The Tenant* (1976), the former being probably the cinema's most intimate, chilling portrayal of madness. *Macbeth* (1971) and *Chinatown* have an overwhelming sense of evil. *Macbeth* is a prolonged bloodbath unleashed by Satanic forces; *Chinatown* is a profound modernist study of the limitless horrors people are capable of in the pursuit of power. *Tess* (1979), an adaptation of Thomas Hardy's *Tess of the d'Urbervilles*, is dedicated "To Sharon", but it is also, one feels, an apologia for Polanski himself, a film about someone victimized through one mistake and hounded by a merciless social law.

Alien visions

In Polanski's films, individuals invariably see themselves as vulnerable aliens in hostile territory, a feeling that the director undoubtedly knows. The films are obsessed with knives and with violence that is often extreme, never cathartic. "I'm not a pessimist," Polanski said once, "I'm just serious." This might account for his characteristically enigmatic endings, which leave an audience uncomfortable, uneasy, still on the hook. Yet he has a shrewd nose for commercial success, and is something of a trend-setter. He adds fresh blood to the horror film in *Rosemary's Baby* (1968); seeps cynicism and color into the black-and-white world of the private-eye in *Chinatown*; and breathes fresh life into the filmed literary classics in *Tess*.

His vision of the world, lurching between horror and black comedy, sadism and surrealism, is deeply disturbing. But it cannot be ignored, partly because of its relevance to some of the atrocities of the modern world, partly because of his filmic mastery. "I am neither critic, nor sociologist," he says, "merely cineaste." He is one of the best there is.

91

Nicolas Roeg (1928 -)

When François Truffaut made his famous remark about the imcompatibility between the terms "cinema" and "Britain", he cannot have been thinking of Nicolas Roeg. The most immediately striking thing about Roeg's films is the arresting cinematic style – bold use of slow motion, fragmented narratives, subliminal images, a packed visual and aural surface that engages an audience's attention on more than one level at any given time. His formal audacity and ambitious subjects have led some to describe him, on the basis of only half-a-dozen films, as Britain's greatest living film-maker.

Roeg became a director after working his way from clapper boy to camera-man on such films as Truffaut's *Fahrenheit 451* (1966) and Richard Lester's *Petulia* (1968). His first film (co-directed with Donald Cammell) was *Performance*, made in 1967 but shelved for nearly three years because of censorship problems over its allegedly excessive violence. *Don't Look Now* (1973) also created something of a storm because of its eroticism, and *Eureka* (1983) had its release delayed because of its obscurity. His work can terrify the more timid of distributors and audiences through its explicit sexuality, furious emotions and technical demands. In his general air of a man possessed, Roeg strikes one as the D.H. Lawrence of the modern cinema.

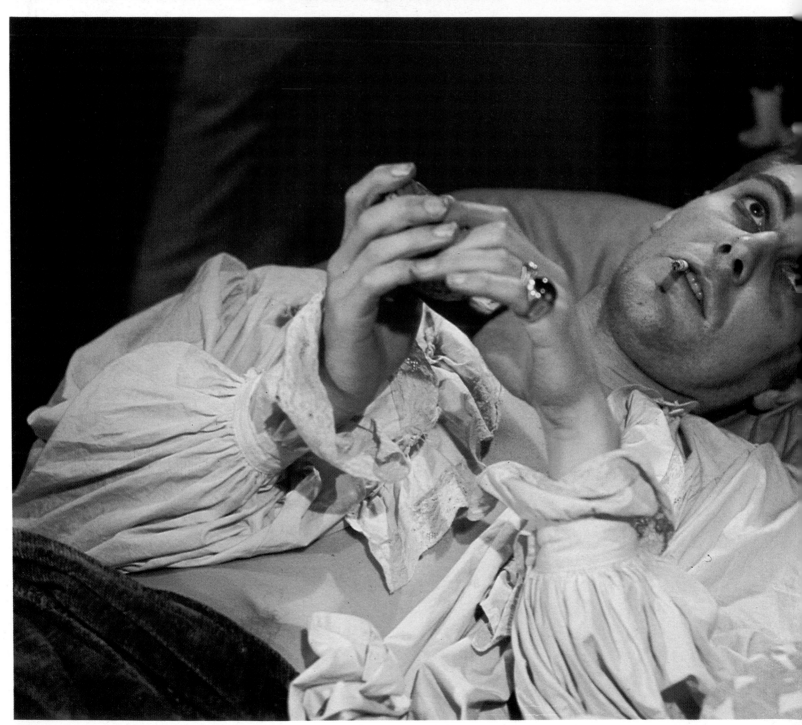

The basic situation of a Roeg film is nearly always identical. The leading character is suddenly thrust into a strange milieu to which he must adjust or from which he must struggle free – what Roeg describes as a "study of what can happen when you step out of your moral background, out of where you are in life". James Fox in *Performance*, Jenny Agutter in *Walkabout* (1971), Donald Sutherland in *Don't Look Now*, Art Garfunkel in *Bad Timing* (1980) all play relatively conservative, emotionally vulnerable people who are suddenly given a glimpse of a more exciting, yet more dangerous world, that puts passion above reason and instinct above intelligence. To pursue this vision could lead to emotional liberation, self-knowledge or, alternatively, madness. Not to pursue it, and stay where you are in life, could result in safety, security but also sterility, frustration, emotional repression.

This is the challenge of a Roeg film and the reason why some people find them uncomfortable and distasteful while others find them literally sensational. He offers a glimpse into another world. *Performance* acts like a hallucinatory drug; *Walkabout* is a sensual rite of passage; *Don't Look Now* gives us all second sight; *The Man Who Fell to Earth* (1976) projects us into a quite alien vision of fallen modern man; *Insignificance* (1985) confronts notions of infinity. When Roeg is at his best, our perceptions are profoundly shaken, and the experience is truly – there is no other word – mind-blowing.

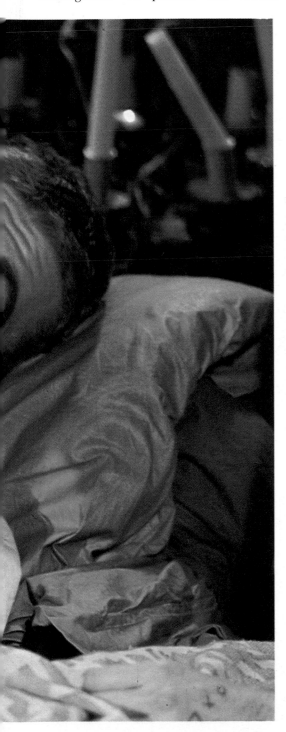

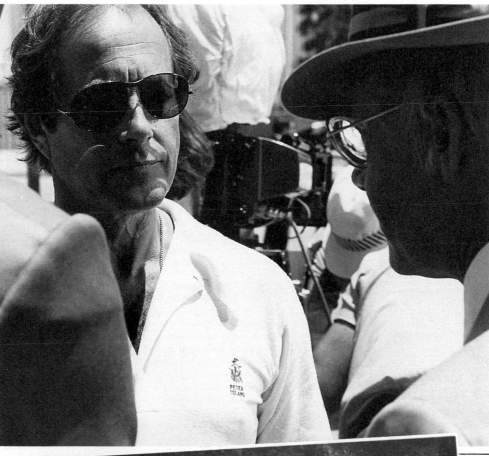

Left: *James Fox as a gangster on the run undergoes a radical transformation in* **Performance** *(1969).*

Top: *Nicholas Roeg (in dark glasses) on set.*

Above: *Gene Hackman as the prospector striking gold in* **Eureka** *(1983).*

Steven Spielberg (1947 -)

The secret of Steven Spielberg's success is his disarming blend of innocence and precociousness. He has the heart of a Peter Pan and the technique of an Alfred Hitchcock. What distinguishes him from some of his contemporaries is that he believes in the film-maker as entertainer more than in the director as ego. Even more distinctively, he seems to believe in the future.

Currently the force is with him. Although not yet 40, he has already made some of the most popular films of all time, including *Jaws* (1975), *Close Encounters of the Third Kind* (1977), *Raiders of the Lost Ark* (1981) and *E.T. – the Extra-Terrestrial* (1982). He is a consummate craftsman but he combines technical flair with enterprising themes and entertaining characterization. If the hero is back with the Indiana Jones films, Spielberg enjoys the moments when he can send up the character, and elsewhere in his films, macho man is satirized, chewed over, parodied and upstaged by the weak. Generally speaking, the strongest relationships in his films are those between mothers and children.

Escape into fantasy

Spielberg has said that his films are basically about ordinary people reacting to extraordinary events. The films begin with an evocation of a recognizable world with which an audience can identify (and he is a shrewd, humorous observer of American suburbia). But the films move logically and audaciously to extravagant adventure, offering not an analysis of modern society but an escape into fantasy. Although there are tremendous moments of suspense in Spielberg's work, notably in *Duel* (1971) and *Jaws*, where man is menaced by a malicious truck and a ravenous shark respectively, the tension approximates to the temporary twinges of the funfair more than the anxieties of real life.

There are some who criticize Spielberg for this, feeling that the insights into character he displayed in *Sugarland Express* (1974) reveal a potential profundity in his work that has not been fulfilled. But, for the vast majority of filmgoers, the escape he provides from the problems of the real world is what the cinema is for, and no less vital to the recession-hit eighties than it was to the Depression-hit thirties. There is no point in asking Spielberg to be Ingmar Bergman when he has made a fortune out of emulating Walt Disney. By bringing magic and fantasy back into the cinema, he has brought mass audiences back into them as well. In Spielberg's future might lie a whole future direction of popular film, but, as yet, he is carrying that responsibility lightly. He shows no sign of losing contact with his public, and they show no sign of losing confidence in him.

Left: *Steven Spielberg and camera crew.*

Bottom left: *The alien spacecraft prepares to land in* **Close Encounters of the Third Kind** *(1977).*

Below: *A menacing moment from the Steven Spielberg production,* **Poltergeist** *(1982), directed by Tobe Hooper.*

Inset: *The shark prepares to attack in* **Jaws** *(1975).*

PICTURE CREDITS